D1236853

A
WORD
TO THE
WISE

A WORD
TO THE
WISE

TRADITIONAL ADVICE AND
OLD COUNTRY WAYS

RUTH BINNEY

DOVER PUBLICATIONS, INC.
Mineola, New York

Copyright

Bibliographical Note

This Dover edition, first published in 2019, is
an unabridged republication of the work originally printed by
Rydon Publishing, West Sussex, England, in 2016.

International Standard Book Number

ISBN-13: 978-0-486-82873-2
ISBN-10: 0-486-82873-5

Manufactured in the United States by LSC Communications
82873501   2019
www.doverpublications.com

CONTENTS

INTRODUCTION

Every year on 22 December – the day after the winter
solstice – I would sit at breakfast, waiting for my father,
a physics teacher, to open his paper, look at the date and
declare that "as the days lengthen the cold strengthens." So
began my interest in old sayings and in science. If we were out together
on a winter's night he would look for a ring round the moon as a sign of
"snow soon" and he often related how, as a child of the Edwardian era,
he would be given on his birthday a maxim to follow for the year ahead
such as "do your duty like a soldier and a man."

The sayings in this book, collected in the years
since my childhood (when we were allowed to
have our hair washed only once a week and schools
gave girls prizes for good deportment), relate closely
to the business of everyday life, largely as it was lived
before the days of modern conveniences, and how they relate
to modern life and knowledge. They include advice on the practical
necessities of cooking, gardening, keeping house and health, as well as
proverbial wisdom concerning good behavior for children, adults, and
life in general.

Many of the old adages that our grandparents believed in have
since been proved true, although others, like putting
butter on a burn, have been discredited. But it is
probably no accident that many once-valuable
items such as salt, eggs and silver recur in the
old sayings, or that they have much to say about
foretelling the weather. For in the days when most

people made their living from the land, being in tune with nature could be vital to survival.

For the superstitious, there are dozens of old country sayings and traditions that relate to good luck, good health and finding a spouse, as well as to omens of disease, death and disaster. Almost everything was once invested with significance, from seeing a single magpie to the day of the week on which you did your washing or cut your nails.

In compiling this book I have used numerous sources old and new, but have drawn particularly on the 19th-century classic advice book *Enquire Within*, a bound-up collection of the magazine *Home Chat* for 1896, *The Concise Household Encyclopedia* of 1933 (discovered at a village fête) and, from America, *The House and Home Practical Book*, also from 1896. I have not, however, tested the old recipes included in the book, so they are used at your own risk.

Many thanks are due to the team at Rydon Publishing, and to my late husband, Donald, for his encouragement in the production of the original book. Together we spent many hours at secondhand bookshops and stalls at home, and in Boston and New York, as he helped me to unearth those invaluable nuggets of reference that have brought this book to life.

Ruth Binney
Dorchester, England, 2016

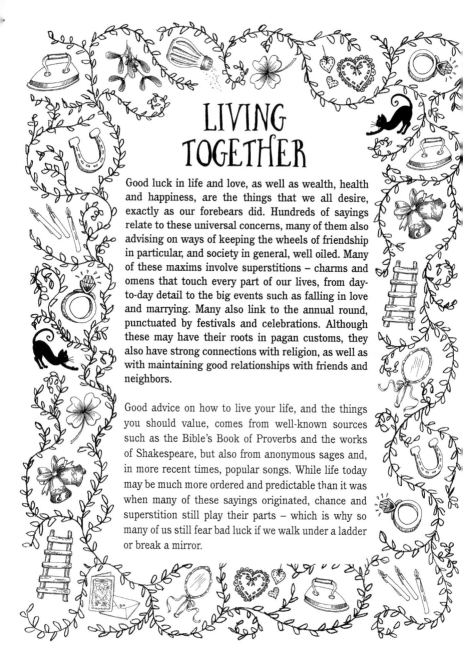

LIVING TOGETHER

Good luck in life and love, as well as wealth, health and happiness, are the things that we all desire, exactly as our forebears did. Hundreds of sayings relate to these universal concerns, many of them also advising on ways of keeping the wheels of friendship in particular, and society in general, well oiled. Many of these maxims involve superstitions – charms and omens that touch every part of our lives, from day-to-day detail to the big events such as falling in love and marrying. Many also link to the annual round, punctuated by festivals and celebrations. Although these may have their roots in pagan customs, they also have strong connections with religion, as well as with maintaining good relationships with friends and neighbors.

Good advice on how to live your life, and the things you should value, comes from well-known sources such as the Bible's Book of Proverbs and the works of Shakespeare, but also from anonymous sages and, in more recent times, popular songs. While life today may be much more ordered and predictable than it was when many of these sayings originated, chance and superstition still play their parts – which is why so many of us still fear bad luck if we walk under a ladder or break a mirror.

BLOW OUT YOUR BIRTHDAY CANDLES WITH ONE BREATH

This is the way, it is said, to make a secret wish come true, but to cry on your birthday is to cry all year. In celebrating birthdays the ancient Greeks honored the birthday of Artemis, goddess of the moon and fertility.

To celebrate the birthday of Artemis the Greeks would light candles on her altar, but her benign favors were granted only if these were blown out with one breath.

Birthdays were probably first celebrated in Egyptian

An iced sponge cake is the traditional children's birthday cake. One recipe dating from 1921 suggests cutting a madeira cake into four layers and putting a different filling between each: strawberry jam, lemon curd and greengage jam.

and Persian households in the 5th century BC, but the birthday cakes and parties of modern times date back only as far as the 19th century. Even then children, while presented with modest gifts, were also treated to lessons in morality and good behavior. Typically, they would be given a saying or motto, such as "Do your duty like a soldier and a man," or "A friend in need is a friend indeed," to live up to in the year ahead.

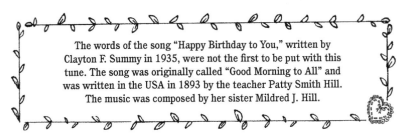

The words of the song "Happy Birthday to You," written by Clayton F. Summy in 1935, were not the first to be put with this tune. The song was originally called "Good Morning to All" and was written in the USA in 1893 by the teacher Patty Smith Hill. The music was composed by her sister Mildred J. Hill.

NEVER SIGN A VALENTINE CARD

Anonymity is an essential element of the cards sent by would-be lovers on February 14. Rather than celebrating one of the little-known saints called Valentine, these romantic tokens probably descend from the traditions of the bawdy pagan fertility festival of early spring, known to the Romans as Lupercalia.

There were several St. Valentines, but two with February 14 as their feast day. Both were Christian martyrs of the 3rd century, one a Roman priest, the other a Roman bishop, although neither is known to have had any connection with love.

In 1723 lovers could refer to **Valentine Writers,** *a book of ready-written verses, for their cards. A century later, Valentine cards had become so popular that postmen demanded additional wages for delivering their increased load.*

The anonymity of a Valentine card stems from the medieval custom (still being practiced in Scotland in the 1860s) that on St. Valentine's eve a woman who was not yet married or betrothed could be won as a bride in the Valentine lottery. This is also thought to be the origin of the superstition that if you are single the first person of the opposite sex you see on the saint's day is your prospective partner.

The practice of sending Valentine cards was begun, it is said, by Charles, duc d'Orléans, when he was imprisoned in the Tower of London following the defeat of the French at the Battle of Agincourt in 1415. However, the first cards decorated with hearts, cupids and lovers' knots were made in the 16th century.

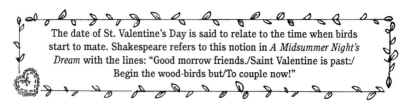

The date of St. Valentine's Day is said to relate to the time when birds start to mate. Shakespeare refers to this notion in *A Midsummer Night's Dream* with the lines: "Good morrow friends./Saint Valentine is past:/Begin the wood-birds but/To couple now!"

DON'T BREAK A MIRROR: YOU'LL HAVE SEVEN YEARS OF BAD LUCK

This is just one of many superstitions about mirrors, which have been prized for more than 7,000 years. While a broken mirror is also said to foretell a death in the family, the proverbial warning to the vain is that too much mirror gazing will make the Devil appear.

It was by polishing the volcanic mineral obsidian that the people of the Middle East and northern Italy made the first mirrors. These were small hand mirrors used during one's personal hygiene. Only when the Venetians discovered how to

The convex mirror featured significantly in Renaissance art, as in Van Eyck's famous painting "The Arnolfini Wedding" where it is thought to represent the observant eye of God.

silver glass in the mid 16th century could large mirrors become expensive decorations for the home; the first patent for their manufacture in Britain was obtained in 1615 by Sir Robert Mansell.

MORE MIRROR SUPERSTITIONS

- ✂ Covering the mirrors, or turning them to the wall, in a room where a dead body is laid out prevents the soul of the departed from being carried off by their ghost.
- ✂ Mirrors must always be covered in a thunderstorm.
- ✂ If a couple first catch sight of each other in a mirror, their relationship will be a happy one.

STRIKE WHILE THE IRON IS HOT

An encouragement to make the most of your opportunities while they last, this saying has its roots in the blacksmith's shop and resonances in the domestic duties carried out in times past.

Since the Iron Age, which began around 1500 BC, heating iron and beating it while red hot into anything from knife blades to plowshares has been central to societies around the world. The smith – and the power of his fire – were much revered in many cultures. According to the ancient Romans, the god Vulcan had his workshop in the fiery heart of Mount Etna in Sicily. Eruptions from the volcano were, they believed, the sparks flying from his smithy, where he made thunderbolts for Jupiter, the ruler of the skies.

Pig iron (iron made in blast furnaces from the 17th century onwards) got its name because, when the molten iron flowing along one large channel ran into many smaller molds leading off at one side, it looked like piglets feeding at the sow.

The first heated domestic irons, which were filled with hot coals, were used in the Far East in the 8th century BC. Box irons of a similar design were used until the 17th century, when solid flatirons, which could be heated directly on the stove, were introduced. Keeping irons hot demanded constant vigilance. If the heat of the stove was allowed to slacken then the irons would be too cool, but the wise housemaid would make sure that she had several "irons in the fire" to cover every eventuality.

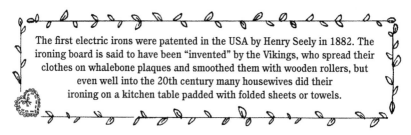

The first electric irons were patented in the USA by Henry Seely in 1882. The ironing board is said to have been "invented" by the Vikings, who spread their clothes on whalebone plaques and smoothed them with wooden rollers, but even well into the 20th century many housewives did their ironing on a kitchen table padded with folded sheets or towels.

WEAR A WEDDING RING ON THE THIRD FINGER OF THE LEFT HAND

••

Although the ancient supposition that the nerve in this finger links directly with the heart is now discredited by accurate studies of anatomy, many people still believe that this positioning of a ring symbolizes the Christian doctrine of the Trinity.

From the Middle Ages it was customary at a wedding for the priest to place the wedding ring over each finger in turn, beginning at the index finger, saying, "In the name of the Father, and of the Son, and of the Holy Ghost, Amen." But the wearing of a wedding ring goes back much further than this. The earliest known have been dated to about 12000 BC, in Sumeria, where they may have evolved from the shackles used – literally – to keep wives in their place.

Once it is on, superstition decrees that the wedding ring should stay firmly in place. Losing a wedding ring is said to symbolize, at best, the loss of a husband's affections. If it is irretrievably mislaid the ring must be replaced, but fortune can only be restored, it is said, if the new one is chosen and paid for by the nearest male members of the wife's family, not by her husband.

Wedding rings for husbands are a relatively new fashion, supplanting the signet ring, traditionally bearing the family crest, worn on the little finger. From ancient times, signet rings were used for signing or sealing documents. The ancient Egyptians wore rings mounted with scarabs (gems cut in the shape of beetles and engraved with symbols on their flat sides) to ward off evil.

YOU CAN'T MAKE AN OMELETTE WITHOUT BREAKING EGGS

A warning that you cannot get something for nothing and that sacrifices, though they may mean effort, can have tangible rewards. The French name betrays the best-known origin of the dish.

*O*n ne saurait faire une omelette sans casser les oeufs is the original French for this expression. The omelette, however, was probably known well before the French coined the word in the 16th century, and has long been enjoyed as a sweet as well as a savory dish. Experts on Middle Eastern food think that it may originally have come from Persia as a more solid dish called an *eggah* – more like a Spanish tortilla, which typically contains potatoes.

Another culinary way of expressing the same thought is the proverb "He who does not kill hogs, will not get black puddings."

On the making of the perfect French omelette, cooks are agreed that the eggs should be very fresh, that they should be cooked in butter, that it is best to keep a special pan for omelette preparation, and that once cooked the omelette should be served immediately. Purists disapprove of the addition of milk advised by the American 19th-century cook Fannie Merritt Farmer. Her "Plain Omelet," known in England as a soufflé omelette, was made by separating the eggs, beating the whites and folding them into the yolks before cooking to give a puffed-up result. The dish was finished in the oven to allow the top to cook through.

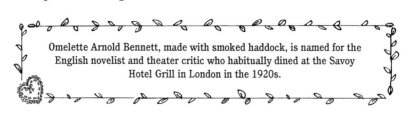

Omelette Arnold Bennett, made with smoked haddock, is named for the English novelist and theater critic who habitually dined at the Savoy Hotel Grill in London in the 1920s.

YOU'LL HAVE GOOD LUCK IF A BLACK CAT CROSSES YOUR PATH

It all depends where you live. Black cats are considered lucky in Britain, when you meet them and also when they enter the house uninvited, but in the USA and mainland Europe they are ill omens. There, it is white felines that are the lucky ones.

The Egyptians revered all cats, whatever their color, for their ability to keep valuable granaries free of rodents. When a cat died it was taken to Bubastis, home of the cat goddess Basht or Pasht, who was also the deity of pleasure and protector against contagious disease, and was believed to have nine lives. Presumably from the sounds of their voices, pet cats were affectionately known as "Mau."

In Europe, cats became the subjects of religious persecution when, in the Middle Ages, they became associated with a form of devil worship in which

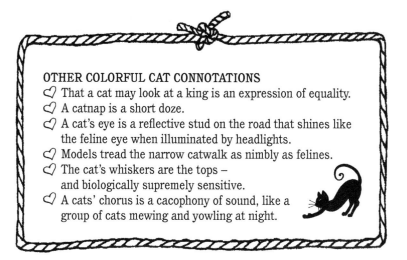

OTHER COLORFUL CAT CONNOTATIONS
- That a cat may look at a king is an expression of equality.
- A catnap is a short doze.
- A cat's eye is a reflective stud on the road that shines like the feline eye when illuminated by headlights.
- Models tread the narrow catwalk as nimbly as felines.
- The cat's whiskers are the tops – and biologically supremely sensitive.
- A cats' chorus is a cacophony of sound, like a group of cats mewing and yowling at night.

> *According to Buddhist lore a rat once ate part of one of the scriptures of the Enlightened One. So the Buddha took a piece of its skin and turned it into a cat. The proof? That rats are still afraid of cats.*

Satan took the form of a black cat. On the plus side, black cats were believed, in Britain, to have considerable powers of healing. Just the touch of a single hair from a black cat's tail would, it was said, cure a sty, while smearing the blood of a black cat on the rash was recommended to clear up an attack of shingles.

KISS AND MAKE UP

The kiss is not just a powerful symbol of reconciliation, probably used in the earliest societies, but also an affectionate greeting and an act of intimacy that is an essential part of being human.

It can be no accident that the kiss is such a potent form of touch. Our lips have evolved, with our hands, as the parts of the body most sensitive to physical contact. And because we smell as we kiss, it is also an act of recognition. As the Bible records, the blind Isaac, as an old man, kissed in blessing the person he thought was his son Esau. But Isaac was mistaken. Instead of Esau he kissed Jacob dressed in his brother's clothes – garments that retained Esau's personal odor.

The kiss of reconciliation may go back even further in our evolution, for, after a quarrel, chimpanzees will kiss and embrace to make the peace. Moreover, some anthropologists, including Desmond Morris, author of *Manwatching* (1977), believe that the French kiss evolved from mothers weaning their children by feeding them mouth-to-mouth with pre-chewed morsels, in an exchange similar to that commonly used by birds and other creatures.

In a whole range of cultures, including Inuit, Maori and Polynesian, nose rubbing or nose kissing is the equivalent of the Western kiss. Describing such behavior among the Malays in the 1830s, Charles Darwin observed, "This lasted rather longer than a cordial shake of the hand with us, and as we vary the force of the

The "kiss of life" is the best way to revive someone who has stopped breathing. It is essential to seal your lips right around the victim's mouth and to pinch their nose closed.

grasp of the hand in shaking, so do they in pressing," and that "during the process they uttered comfortable little grunts." The very act of physical contact, as in a kiss but also in a hug, is said by psychologists to have a calming effect on the brain.

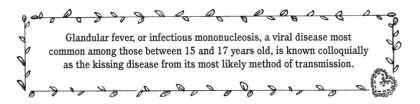

Glandular fever, or infectious mononucleosis, a viral disease most common among those between 15 and 17 years old, is known colloquially as the kissing disease from its most likely method of transmission.

YOU CAN TELL A PERSON'S CHARACTER BY THEIR HANDWRITING

And, say the experts, even more than this, when they analyze both the overall impression of a person's writing style and elements such as the size and shape of the letters and the way in which they are joined and embellished.

Beware, says the American specialist Dr Baruch M. Lazewnik, of a graceful, flowing writing style. Its beautiful appearance can mask a manipulative personality. Equally, he warns against characterizing backward or left-sloping writing as betraying a weak character. Rather, he maintains, it may indicate a tendency to pull back from emotional attachments. A marked slant to the right, however, is agreed by many graphologists to indicate an extrovert.

Other keys to character in handwriting are angles – the connecting strokes used most often by analytical thinkers – and the loops and flourishes favored by more artistic personalities. The way in which letters are joined – or not – is a guide to the way a person uses logic and connects thoughts and ideas. A tense person may write with great pressure, giving the pen strokes little variation in light and shade.

Police forces around the world use graphology experts to detect forgeries, especially signatures, which are particularly difficult to identify if the forger has successfully managed to mimic a victim's writing habits.

It was not just the quality of handwriting that was stressed in the 1933 *News Chronicle* guide to letter writing for housewives. It also maintained that: "You can read character in the trouble that has been taken to form a pleasant phrase, kindness in some happy little thought, and pride and self-respect in clear, legible writing and the way the epistle is set out."

WALKING UNDER LADDERS BRINGS BAD LUCK

Apart from the obvious risk of having something fall on you, the association between ladders and misfortune also goes back to the old practice of hanging criminals – particularly at Tyburn in London – by making them climb a ladder to the gallows.

Some people also believe that a ladder placed against a wall is unlucky because it forms a triangle with the wall and the ground – a sign for the Trinity (Father, Son and Holy Ghost) – and so is sacred.

Accidents with ladders are commonplace. In Britain about 50 people

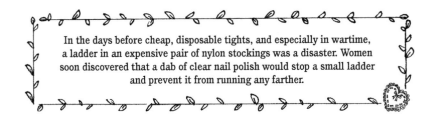

In the days before cheap, disposable tights, and especially in wartime, a ladder in an expensive pair of nylon stockings was a disaster. Women soon discovered that a dab of clear nail polish would stop a small ladder and prevent it from running any farther.

a year are killed by them and over 30,000 need hospital treatment. A household guide published in the 1930s advised that when raising or lowering a long ladder the "amateur should, in all cases of doubt, attach a strong rope to the top of the ladder so it can be controlled."

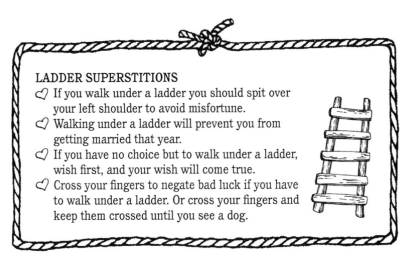

LADDER SUPERSTITIONS

- If you walk under a ladder you should spit over your left shoulder to avoid misfortune.
- Walking under a ladder will prevent you from getting married that year.
- If you have no choice but to walk under a ladder, wish first, and your wish will come true.
- Cross your fingers to negate bad luck if you have to walk under a ladder. Or cross your fingers and keep them crossed until you see a dog.

THROW SPILLED SALT OVER YOUR SHOULDER

It is testament to salt's great value that its spilling should herald ill luck. But, fortunately for the clumsy, it has been a long-held belief that throwing salt over your shoulder can act as an effective antidote.

Ancient suspicions surrounding spilled salt agree that it can bring on all kinds of disaster – from a fallen roof to a fatal wound. Its association with misfortune is thought by some to originate from the depiction by Leonardo da Vinci, in "The Last Supper," of the traitor Judas turning over the salt cellar.

The original salt cellar was a large bowl or "saler" placed in the center of the table. In the 16th and 17th centuries the bowl was replaced by large "steeple" cellars made of silver, crystal or some other valuable material and often decorated with gold or even precious stones.

The word salary *comes from the salt ration or* salarium *given by the Romans to soldiers and civil servants.*

The use of numerous small salt cellars on a large dining table came into vogue after about 1700. Even in the early 20th century etiquette still called for one salt cellar (with a pepper pot) to be set at every other place for a formal dinner so that no one need suffer the indignity of having to ask their neighbor to pass the salt. The practice remains today for the most formal dinners, such as those put on by royalty for visiting dignitaries.

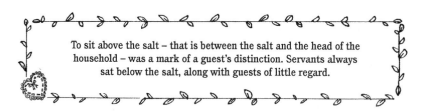

To sit above the salt – that is between the salt and the head of the household – was a mark of a guest's distinction. Servants always sat below the salt, along with guests of little regard.

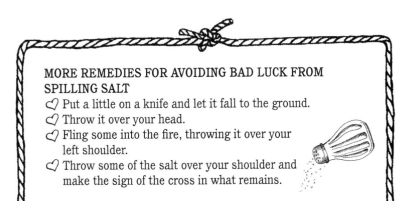

MORE REMEDIES FOR AVOIDING BAD LUCK FROM
SPILLING SALT

♌ Put a little on a knife and let it fall to the ground.
♌ Throw it over your head.
♌ Fling some into the fire, throwing it over your
   left shoulder.
♌ Throw some of the salt over your shoulder and
   make the sign of the cross in what remains.

NEVER LOOK A GIFT HORSE IN THE MOUTH

This proverbial advice on gratitude has its origins in the time-honored
practice of judging a horse's age by its teeth. As a horse ages its gums
recede at a steady rate, making the creature literally "long in the tooth."

An adult horse with its full dentition has between 36 and 40 teeth. On
either side of each jaw are three incisors or "cutting teeth" and six
molars or "grinders," in front of which is a gap where the bit is placed
inside the horse's mouth. Males also have
four small canines or "dog teeth."

> *The horse is a symbol of
> courage, which makes it no
> accident that St. George is
> always depicted on horseback.*

Within two weeks of its birth a foal
develops "nippers," or central teeth, and a
full set of milk teeth (shed during the third
year) is in place by six months. The males
acquire their canines in the fourth year and the set of permanent teeth is
complete by the age of six. At seven years old a hook begins to show on the
corner incisors on the upper jaw and at eight a "dental star" appears on the
central incisors.

Thereafter it becomes more difficult to age a horse, but experts look for "Galvayne's grooves," dark markings on the incisors that appear at the age of ten and reach all the way down the corner teeth by the time the animal is 20.

Unlike human teeth, a horse's molars have evolved to carry on growing as fast as they wear down at the crowns. This is an adaptation to a diet of grass, because the sharp silica it contains rapidly destroys tooth enamel.

DIAMONDS ARE A GIRL'S BEST FRIEND

The saying immortalized by the actress Marilyn Monroe in the 1953 movie *Gentlemen Prefer Blondes* is an apt expression of the real and legendary value of these most precious gems.

The song, written in 1949 by Leo Robin and set to music by Jule Styne, became Monroe's "signature tune" and includes the famous lines:

A kiss on the hand may be quite continental
but diamonds are a girl's best friend,
A kiss may be grand but it won't pay the rental
on your humble flat,
or help you at the automat.
Men grow cold as girls grow old
and we all lose our charms in the end
But square-cut or pear-shaped
these rocks don't lose their shape.
Diamonds are a girl's best friend.

Diamonds certainly don't lose their shape. An isotope (form) of carbon, they are the hardest natural materials we know. They are ancient, too; the youngest were formed 70 million years ago, although they were first discovered around the 4th millennium BC when plucked from Indian riverbeds. Until the volcanic rocks of Kimberley, South Africa, began to yield up their gems in 1870, all diamonds were extracted from sand and gravel. At first diamonds were simply polished to a shine. Cutting them into shapes with brilliantly reflective facets began in the 15th century, and in 1477 Archduke Maximilian of Austria (destined to become the Holy Roman Emperor) began the tradition of the diamond engagement ring with the promissory token he presented to his fiancée Mary of Burgundy.

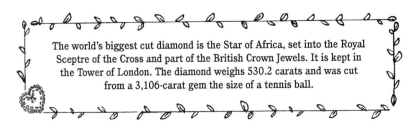

The world's biggest cut diamond is the Star of Africa, set into the Royal Sceptre of the Cross and part of the British Crown Jewels. It is kept in the Tower of London. The diamond weighs 530.2 carats and was cut from a 3,106-carat gem the size of a tennis ball.

DON'T WEAR GREEN AT WEDDINGS

Green is an unlucky color – after green, it is said, comes black. The belief may come from the association of green with the mischief wrought by green-clad elves and fairies.

According to William Henderson's *Notes on the Folk Lore of the Northern Counties of England and the Borders* of 1866, nothing green should appear at a wedding, and even "kale and all other green vegetables"

The new husband carries his wife across the threshold to avoid the bad luck of stumbling at the entrance to her new home.

should be excluded from the wedding dinner. Blue, by contrast, is a lucky color, for as the traditional verse goes: "Those dressed in blue have lovers true; in green and white, forsaken quite." Blue is the color of the sky and of healing, and is also worn by a baby boy (see Choose Pink for a Girl, Blue for a Boy).

Warding off evil spirits at weddings in particular, and in life in general, has a long tradition. Fairies are believed to enter a house down the chimney or through a keyhole at night and harm the people sleeping in a house. Elves were believed to kill animals by throwing "elf-shot" – stones that embedded themselves into the creatures and killed them.

OTHER ILL OMENS TO AVOID ON WEDDING DAYS
- The bride and groom seeing each other before they meet at church.
- The bride bursting a seam on her dress (this means she will be ill-treated by her husband).
- The wedding party meeting a funeral cortege on the way to or from the church.
- Marrying in Lent.
- A dog passing between the couple.
- An open grave in the churchyard.
- The bride wearing new shoes.

KISS UNDER THE MISTLETOE

The white-berried plant cherished since ancient times for its magical powers is still hung up at Christmas and New Year for luck and love. Tradition dictates that with each kiss a man should remove one berry and put it in his pocket or buttonhole. On production of the berry he can then claim more kisses on demand.

"Mistletoe," said the Roman writer Pliny in his *Natural History* of AD 77, "will promote conception in females if they make a practice of carrying it about them," and the mistletoe's long-held connection with fertility is undoubtedly one of the reasons why couples kiss

Mistletoe was often dried and kept for good luck in every season, but because of its pagan associations, churches still discourage the use of mistletoe in Christmas decorations.

beneath it. Mistletoe has also been believed for centuries to be a potent antidote to witchcraft and even the Devil himself. Its magical powers have particular associations with the Druids, the priests of the ancient Celtic tribes, who used it in enacting their devotions, especially at Yule, a pagan midwinter festival marked by indulgent eating and drinking.

In winter, you can see great swathes of mistletoe (*Viscum album*) hanging in orchards on the bare branches of apple trees, and from tall limes and poplars, its leaves shaped like coat hangers and its white berries glistening in the pale sunshine. This partial parasite has no roots, and relies for many of its nutrients on the tree that is its host. The male and female flowers are borne on separate plants: only the females produce the valued fruits.

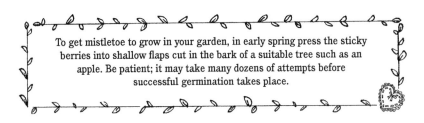

To get mistletoe to grow in your garden, in early spring press the sticky berries into shallow flaps cut in the bark of a suitable tree such as an apple. Be patient; it may take many dozens of attempts before successful germination takes place.

MANNERS MAKETH MAN - AND WOMAN TOO

Although the addendum to the saying is modern, the first part of it comes from a 15th-century book of manners, *The Babees' Book*. Rules for good behavior, however, can be traced back to the earliest civilizations.

B e prudent when you open your mouth," said the Egyptian Pharaoh in his *Instructions* written around 2000 BC, a treatise that laid down the first known rules of manners. Much later, etiquette evolved with the rules of precedence established in Anglo-Saxon courts of the 10th century and, especially in the three centuries that followed, with the ideal of chivalry – encompassing service, protection of individuals, and fidelity – that was enacted by knights who fought in the Crusades.

Historically, a gentleman was a man of good (that is, high) birth, and his wife was automatically a lady. But because the rank of gentleman could be acquired through both wealth and landowning, as well as by noble deeds, the distinction between status and manners became, and has remained, blurred. By the 19th century the rules of good manners were strongly tilted towards the likes and dislikes of the middle class rather than the aristocracy. Examples included: "Be affable and studious to please"; "Avoid drunkenness"; "Beware of foppery and flirtation"; and "Prefer to listen than to talk."

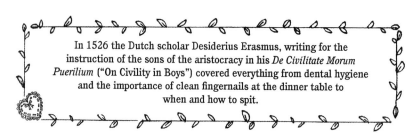

In 1526 the Dutch scholar Desiderius Erasmus, writing for the instruction of the sons of the aristocracy in his *De Civilitate Morum Puerilium* ("On Civility in Boys") covered everything from dental hygiene and the importance of clean fingernails at the dinner table to when and how to spit.

BEAUTY IS IN THE EYE OF THE BEHOLDER

Meaning that, whether skin deep or not, beauty is purely subjective, especially to the lovelorn and proud parents. Mathematics may have the last word, however, for many of the world's most beautiful objects obey the rules of the golden ratio.

The golden ratio works like this. Take any two numbers and add them together (say 10 + 9). Then add the result (19) to the second number (9 + 19 = 28). Then do the same again (19 + 28 = 47). Whatever the sequence, the ratio of the last two numbers is close to the golden ratio of 1.618; beyond the decimal point there is always an infinite string of numbers. Without being aware of it, we judge the appearance of objects by the closeness with which their proportions approximate to the golden ratio.

If you don't think you're beautiful don't worry, for all cats, they say, are gray in the dark!

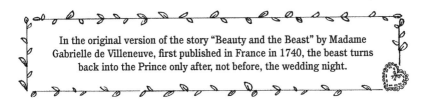

In the original version of the story "Beauty and the Beast" by Madame Gabrielle de Villeneuve, first published in France in 1740, the beast turns back into the Prince only after, not before, the wedding night.

MAKE NEW YEAR'S RESOLUTIONS

New Year is a time for ringing out the old and ringing in the new, not just with resolutions but also with customs deemed to bring wealth and good fortune for another twelve months.

The New Year theme of atonement, still strongly upheld in the Jewish tradition, probably dates back, for Christian societies, to the fact that in the Middle Ages New Year was originally celebrated on March 25, around the time of Easter. Today we resolve to eat and drink less – or to change our lives more radically – but when times were harder, New Year's superstitions were focused more strongly on assuring prosperity.

In Scotland, where New Year or Hogmanay is celebrated with great vigor, it was the custom to take a dog to the door, give him a piece of bread, then drive him away with the words, "Get away you dog." With his expulsion all the ills of a family were deemed to have departed with him.

For luck, the first-footer – the first person arriving at any home on New Year's Day – should be a dark-haired man and should bring with him a lump of coal. Symbolically, this is to keep the fire going. If it goes out, good fortune, it is said, will be extinguished for the rest of the coming year.

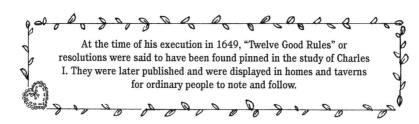

At the time of his execution in 1649, "Twelve Good Rules" or resolutions were said to have been found pinned in the study of Charles I. They were later published and were displayed in homes and taverns for ordinary people to note and follow.

MORE NEW YEAR SUPERSTITIONS

- ♡ Open all the doors on the stroke of midnight to let the old year out.
- ♡ Don't lend anything on New Year's Day or you will be lending all year.
- ♡ It's bad luck to break something on New Year's Day.
- ♡ The first-footer must come in by the back door and leave the house by the front door.
- ♡ For wealth, put coins in everyone's pockets, including those of children.
- ♡ Don't throw ashes out of the house, as they may land on Christ's face and bring bad luck.
- ♡ Don't wash clothes on New Year's Day; if you do, you wash a family member away.

SLEEP ON IT

This advice is now proven to be a rapid and effective means of problem-solving but it was long held anecdotally to be the surest way of soothing worries as well as refreshing both body and mind.

Between 1909 and 1916 the Reverend Nehemiah Curnock, an English parson, published eight volumes in which he deciphered the 18th-century *Journal* of John Wesley, the founder of Methodism, which was originally written in code. Having bought a Bible annotated in the same code, he studied it for days, but had no success in finding the solution. Then one night he dreamed that he was reading the "clear" deciphered text and, when he awoke, found that he had cracked the code.

January 2004 saw the publication of studies by a group of German scientists working in Cologne and Lubeck who devised an elegant experiment to prove the saying. First they sent trained volunteers a math problem that could be solved in seven steps or, using a neat shortcut, in only three. Having been presented with the task, some volunteers were allowed to sleep, others were not. Eight hours later, 13 of the 22 people who had slept worked out the shortcut compared with 5 of the 22 who had not.

The key, say the experts, is that sleep reorganizes information in the brain, but for problem-solving it has been discovered that REM (rapid eye movement) sleep, during which dreams are most likely to occur, is crucial. Certainly many creative people do their best work early in the morning. Samuel Taylor Coleridge claimed to have written the poem "Kubla Khan" in its entirety having woken after opium-induced slumber.

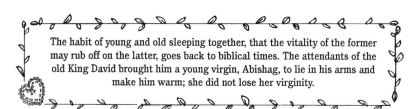

The habit of young and old sleeping together, that the vitality of the former may rub off on the latter, goes back to biblical times. The attendants of the old King David brought him a young virgin, Abishag, to lie in his arms and make him warm; she did not lose her virginity.

WHEN SOMEONE SNEEZES, SAY "BLESS YOU"

A guard against ill fortune – including illness – that goes back at least to Roman times, and is echoed in the German expression *gesundheit*, meaning "health."

In the children's nursery rhyme "Ring a Ring o' Roses" the sneeze epitomizes the symptoms of the Black Death that swept through Europe between 1348 and 1351 – hence "atishoo, atishoo we all fall down." And although some people attribute the origin of the custom to St. Gregory, the Greeks used a similar expression at the time of the Athenian plague. "Bless you" was also employed by the Roman author Apuleius in *The Golden Ass* (translated by Robert Graves): " 'Bless you, my dear!' he said and 'bless you, bless you!' at the second and third sneeze."

As well as the obvious association between sneezing and disease, another reason for acknowledging a sneeze is the superstition that when a person sneezes their soul flies out of their body. A blessing at that moment prevents the Devil from taking the place of the soul before it can get back in.

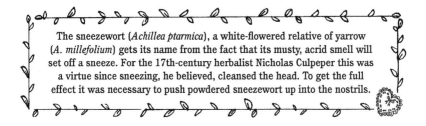

The sneezewort (*Achillea ptarmica*), a white-flowered relative of yarrow (*A. millefolium*) gets its name from the fact that its musty, acrid smell will set off a sneeze. For the 17th-century herbalist Nicholas Culpeper this was a virtue since sneezing, he believed, cleansed the head. To get the full effect it was necessary to push powdered sneezewort up into the nostrils.

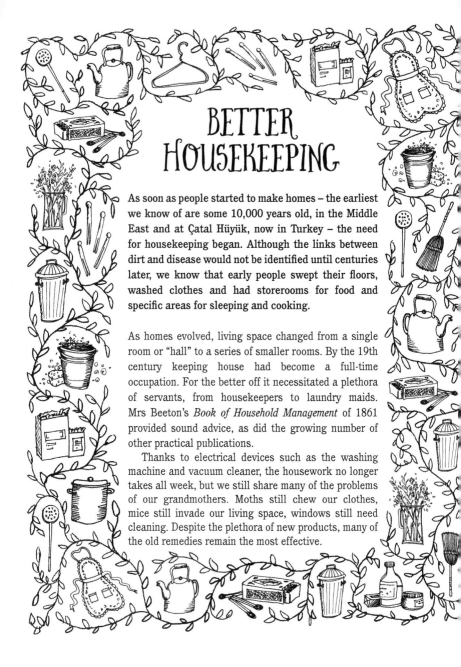

BETTER HOUSEKEEPING

As soon as people started to make homes – the earliest we know of are some 10,000 years old, in the Middle East and at Çatal Hüyük, now in Turkey – the need for housekeeping began. Although the links between dirt and disease would not be identified until centuries later, we know that early people swept their floors, washed clothes and had storerooms for food and specific areas for sleeping and cooking.

As homes evolved, living space changed from a single room or "hall" to a series of smaller rooms. By the 19th century keeping house had become a full-time occupation. For the better off it necessitated a plethora of servants, from housekeepers to laundry maids. Mrs Beeton's *Book of Household Management* of 1861 provided sound advice, as did the growing number of other practical publications.

Thanks to electrical devices such as the washing machine and vacuum cleaner, the housework no longer takes all week, but we still share many of the problems of our grandmothers. Moths still chew our clothes, mice still invade our living space, windows still need cleaning. Despite the plethora of new products, many of the old remedies remain the most effective.

DE-SCALE A KETTLE WITH VINEGAR

The classroom chemistry of acid plus alkali is the secret behind this effective tip, which is sure to save you money on any expensive proprietary preparations. Lemon juice also works well in both kettles and showerheads.

L imescale, made primarily of alkaline calcium carbonate, is deposited as "fur" in your kettle (and dishwasher, washing machine and toilet) if you live in a hard water area. Dissolved calcium compounds separate out as the water is boiled, and eventually accumulate as solid lumps.

Vinegar, which is acetic acid (or lemon juice, which is citric acid) reacts with limescale and dissolves it. For bad scaling, fill the kettle with a mixture of malt or white pickling vinegar diluted half and half with water, bring it to the boil and leave it

Among thieves, 'kettle' is slang for a stolen watch. A tin-kettle denotes a silver one, while a red-kettle is gold.

for a couple of hours or overnight. If any furring remains, simply repeat the process.

A small piece of wire mesh inside a kettle will collect "fur." A similar old remedy is recommended by *Enquire Within*. To remove an "unpleasant crust," it advises placing "a clean oyster-shell or a piece of stone or marble" within, which "will always keep the interior of the kettle in good order, by attracting the particles of earth or of stone."

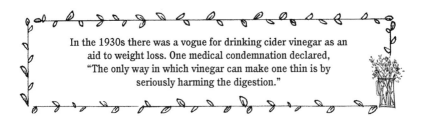

In the 1930s there was a vogue for drinking cider vinegar as an aid to weight loss. One medical condemnation declared, "The only way in which vinegar can make one thin is by seriously harming the digestion."

USE LAVENDER TO KEEP CLOTHES MOTHS AT BAY

Lavender will keep your drawers and wardrobes smelling sweet, but as a moth deterrent it is not nearly as effective as some traditionalists would have you believe. For a natural choice, cedar oil is a better remedy, but is still far from totally reliable.

The clothes moth (*Tineola bisselliella*) is a menace. It lays its eggs on the fibres of clothes and carpets, where they hatch into larvae about ¼ inch (6 mm) long, which then plump themselves up by munching holes in your prized garments and furnishings. Wool is their favorite food, but they will also devour cotton and even leather and fur. The moths that hatch from the larvae don't eat at all, but are ready to mate and restart the cycle.

In northern England clothes moths are sometimes known as 'ghosts'. Killing one is thought to precipitate the death of a relative.

Camphor oil was the original ingredient of mothballs, but has been superseded by more powerful and effective chemicals, such as naphthalene and parachlorobenzene. If you use them, follow any instructions to the letter.

Cleanliness was, and is, the most effective way of protecting items from moths, which are particularly attracted to food and grease on clothes. Keeping woolens well brushed (skin flakes are additional food) will help them stay moth-free, and ironing may kill the eggs.

The 1920s housewife was advised to get rid of carpet moths by scrubbing the floor with "hot water made exceedingly salty before replacing the carpet, and sprinkle the carpet once a week before sweeping until the pests disappear." The beating of rugs, a household duty now replaced by vacuuming, was a standard part of the weekly cleaning routine.

SET A CAT TO CATCH A MOUSE

• •

The ancient Egyptians kept cats in their granaries to kill mice and rats. Some 3,500 years on, felines are still effective against these household pests, although a really bad rodent infestation may require the intervention of a professional controller.

Cat versus mouse is a matter of instinct. A cat is "programmed" to chase and torment a mouse (or a fluff-filled replica or even a rolled-up pair of socks until it tires of the deception), and while a pet cat may present you with dead rodents as "gifts," its untamed ancestors would have relied on these creatures for food. And although a cat will hunt during the day, at heart it is a night hunter, using its natural attributes of reflective eyes, acute hearing, sensitive whiskers, sharp claws and long canine teeth to detect and seize its prey. Cats also have the patience to wait for hours for their prey and to torment it until it is finally dead.

Mice rely for their evolutionary success on safety in numbers (ensured by rapid and persistent breeding), agility and an omnivorous diet that can even include newspapers and electric cables. They are also intelligent enough to work out how to avoid the most cunning mousetraps and all but the most tempting of chemical baits.

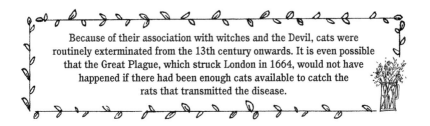

Because of their association with witches and the Devil, cats were routinely exterminated from the 13th century onwards. It is even possible that the Great Plague, which struck London in 1664, would not have happened if there had been enough cats available to catch the rats that transmitted the disease.

MOUSE-CATCHING TIPS
If you can't or won't keep a cat, try one of these methods of catching or deterring mice:

- Block up their exits and entrances, including the smallest gaps under doors, between floorboards and around pipes.
- Smear mint toothpaste round the edges of their holes; the smell will deter them.
- Bait mousetraps with bacon, peanut butter or nut chocolate rather than cheese.
- Put down proprietary mousekiller, but be sure to keep poisons away from food and children. Handle any deceased animals wearing rubber gloves.

NEVER EAT A BOILED EGG WITH A SILVER SPOON

The quickest way to tarnish silver is to use it to eat an egg. Not only that, the reaction between the silver and the egg can create a foul taste in the mouth. Vegetables high in sulfur, such as cabbage, will also tarnish silver.

When silver comes in contact with hydrogen sulphide, the "bad eggs" gas that dissipates from a yolk forms blue-black silver sulphide, or tarnish. Washing up directly after a meal will help prevent tarnishing, and for taking a little tarnish off sterling silver the quickest and easiest remedy is to soak it in hot water to which you have added a teaspoon of dishwashing soap or baking soda.

For a high shine, you can buff silver with a cloth or a chamois leather, but this risks wearing away the coating of EPS or "silver plate." To treat a heavy tarnish the experts advise against immersing silver in an acid "dip."

A jeweler's rouge cloth is the nearest modern equivalent to the old method of cleaning silver. In former times the rouge would have been bought as a powder and mixed with ammonia before use.

If used at all, apply it sparingly on a sponge soaked in the solution and wash it off in very hot water immediately afterwards.

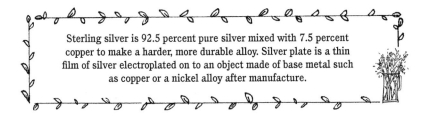

Sterling silver is 92.5 percent pure silver mixed with 7.5 percent copper to make a harder, more durable alloy. Silver plate is a thin film of silver electroplated on to an object made of base metal such as copper or a nickel alloy after manufacture.

DON'T DRY WET SHOES BY THE FIRE

Soaked leather, if dried quickly, will become brittle and cracked and develop white "tide marks." The old way is still the best way: sponge wet shoes, stuff them with crumpled newspaper and leave them to dry slowly and naturally in the air.

There is nothing more frustrating than having a good pair of shoes ruined by rain or snow, and an old way of waterproofing them was to rub them with castor oil or petroleum jelly or with a mixture of beeswax and lard. Paraffin oil was added to boot blacking to protect and restore damp leather, while varnishing the soles of boots was said to "render them impervious to damp and make them last longer."

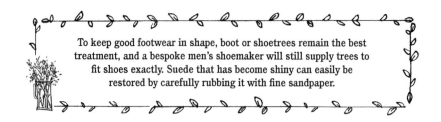

To keep good footwear in shape, boot or shoetrees remain the best treatment, and a bespoke men's shoemaker will still supply trees to fit shoes exactly. Suede that has become shiny can easily be restored by carefully rubbing it with fine sandpaper.

In the days before mass manufacture, leather boots and shoes were particularly valuable items. Durable clogs, with iron-shod wooden soles and leather or fabric uppers, were a cheaper and more hard-wearing alternative for most working people in Britain. In the Netherlands and other continental European countries, all-wood clogs were worn. In wartime Britain – and in post-war years when clothes were still rationed – it was commonplace for children to have a single pair of shoes for the winter from which the toes were cut to make "sandals" for the summer.

It is said that in autumn the best way to dry out damp shoes is to fill them with chopped horse chestnuts.

POLISH WINDOWS WITH NEWSPAPER

Rolled into a pad, newspaper is a good old-fashioned substitute for a polishing cloth or chamois leather, but it is by no means the only effective way to get the shine on your panes that was once essential to a good reputation. "Dirty windows," it was said, "speak to the passer-by of the negligence of the inmates."

Dirty windows not only deprive rooms of light but make them look unattractive. If you can, clean the windows on a dull day, or at least when the sun is not shining on the glass, to prevent streaks and allow you to see the results of your labors clearly.

Good modern cleaning choices are either washing with a solution of detergent or a proprietary liquid, or using a spray containing ammonia and alcohol, which then needs to be rubbed off with a soft cloth. The squeegee, used by the professionals, is an excellent – and

Despite its name, chamois leather is not made from goatskin but from the underlayer or "split" of a sheepskin after the top layer of skin has been removed.

some say the only – means of getting a sparkling finish on your windows.

Don't forget the frames. Regular dusting helps to keep them free of dirt, but in winter it is also essential to remove any condensation that accumulates on them: as well as rotting wooden frames, it can be the breeding ground for unsightly black mildew.

OLD WINDOW-CLEANING RECIPES

- ⊛ Equal parts of paraffin and methylated spirits rubbed on to dry glass and polished off when dry.
- ⊛ A bunch of stinging nettles dipped into water with a dash of vinegar added (wear thick gloves!). Dry the glass with a soft cloth or chamois.
- ⊛ Turpentine: especially good for grease marks.
- ⊛ A solution made by pouring boiling water on a chopped potato.
- ⊛ Washing soda dissolved in water, with a little ammonia added.

BEWARE OF ONE BAD APPLE IN THE BARREL

For the prudent housekeeper, a warning that, without regular checks on the health of the crop, brown rot will gradually spread from fruit to fruit in winter storage. For life, a warning that one disruptive person can cause havoc within a whole group.

Apples rot on the outside because they are attacked by a fungus. This often enters at a "weak spot" created if the fruit is eaten by caterpillars (the tortrix moth is a common attacker). Spreading areas of brown on the skin are typically topped with blotches or rings of white fungal spores.

In the Bible, the book of Genesis does not specify the apple as the forbidden fruit in the Garden of Eden. In fact it was probably a fig.

The autumn apple crop from the garden or orchard should keep well into spring if disease-free fruit is carefully picked to ensure that it is not bruised and sympathetically stored in a cool, dry, well-ventilated place. Ideally the temperature should not fall below 37°F (3°C).

Barrels were the traditional storage vessels for apples, although in the country large quantities were also layered between straw in massive heaps. For even better keeping, store apples so that they do not touch one another. Ideal for the purpose are large greengrocers' fiber fruit trays, or plastic or cardboard trays in which apples wrapped individually in tissue paper or newspaper can be embedded in coir "compost."

As a rule, the later an apple matures the longer it will keep. Varieties to choose for storing include Bramley's Seedling and Howgate Wonder (cookers) and Cox's Orange Pippin and Golden Delicious (eaters). But there are lots of other ways to keep apples, including windfalls, from old-fashioned apple butters and chutneys to apple sauces, pies and charlottes, which will keep for months in the freezer.

GET GREASE MARKS OFF CLOTHES BY IRONING THEM OVER BLOTTING PAPER

The theory is that the heat of the iron will melt the grease – on carpets as well as clothes – which will then be absorbed by the blotting paper. In practice, however, if you try this you need to be careful you don't "cook" the mark and make it even more difficult to remove.

For washable clothes, the best way to get rid of grease marks (made by anything from mayonnaise to machine oil) is to rub them with liquid detergent then wash them with detergent in the hottest water possible. Pre-wash treatment with a proprietary stain remover may help, but be sure to test the fabric first to make sure that it is colourfast. Take anything that can't be washed to the dry cleaners and highlight the offending areas for special treatment. For carpets and rugs, carpet shampoos are most effective, either for spot cleaning of grease stains or all-over cleaning.

On grease, detergents are much more effective than soap because they not only act to emulsify the fat – break it up into minute droplets that will then lift off the fibers of a fabric – but, as they do so, attach themselves selectively to dirt. The first detergents were developed in Germany in the 1880s, and Nekal was the first brand name detergent, sold there in 1917. However in the days before detergents, another recommended method was to rub dry flour on a garment or carpet and to leave it for several hours to absorb any grease or oil. Turpentine was also used as a dry cleaner.

Candle wax can be more easily scraped off if it is first hardened with a block of ice. The remains can then be given the hot iron and blotting paper treatment.

POLISH FURNITURE WITH BEESWAX

Natural beeswax from the hive is still one of the best polishes for keeping wooden furniture in great condition, although special finishes need other kinds of treatment.

Waxing and polishing furniture protects it and keeps it looking shiny and bright. It won't need re-treating more than once or twice a year, depending on how often it is used. Once well waxed, with a bought or homemade polish (see below) it can be cleaned with a duster (aided if you wish by a proprietary dusting spray) or wiped with a barely damp cloth. Furniture finished with shellac, lacquer or varnish is better left unwaxed. Soapy water used sparingly on a soft cloth should remove all but the worst marks.

You can make a good all-purpose beeswax mixture at home by melting 2 tablespoons of beeswax granules with the same quantity of turpentine. Oak furniture that is stained or dull will take on a wonderful shine if polished with a warm mixture of 1 tablespoon of beeswax granules melted with ½ pint (300 ml) beer and 2 teaspoons of sugar.

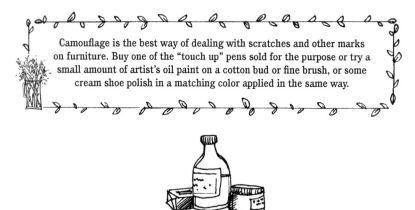

Camouflage is the best way of dealing with scratches and other marks on furniture. Buy one of the "touch up" pens sold for the purpose or try a small amount of artist's oil paint on a cotton bud or fine brush, or some cream shoe polish in a matching color applied in the same way.

MAKE DO AND MEND

In the days before cheap clothes and hard-wearing artificial fibers, mending was a necessity. And until the late 20th century, home dressmaking was an essential part of "making do" for all but the wealthy.

Darning – especially of socks and stockings, which wore out quickly – was an almost daily necessity in the days before the invention of nylon and polyester. To make the task easier, a wooden darning ball, egg or mushroom was put inside and the area containing the hole stretched smoothly over it.

With the ever-increasing demands of fashion, which reached their height in the late 1800s, came an even greater need for frugality. Mending was essential for a respectable middle class woman who needed six different outfits for just an ordinary day – typically a

The first metal needles for sewing were made in the Middle East and brought to Europe in the 14th century. Early metal needles made in Germany in 1370 had a hook at one end to keep the thread in place.

dressing gown, a "costume" or suit for shopping, a day dress (and an overall for kitchen work), an afternoon dress, a tea gown and a dress for dinner – plus all the extras to go with them, from trimmed bonnets to kid gloves.

Young married women would also make their husband's shirts and stockings and the advent of paper patterns was a boon for the thrifty housewife. During the 19th century, women's magazines produced patterns that needed to be copied and enlarged by hand from the page, but the big breakthrough came when the American tailor Ebenezer Butterick began selling ready-sized packaged paper patterns.

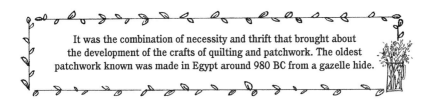

It was the combination of necessity and thrift that brought about the development of the crafts of quilting and patchwork. The oldest patchwork known was made in Egypt around 980 BC from a gazelle hide.

TURN YOUR MATTRESS ONCE A MONTH

The reasoning behind mattress turning is to prevent sagging in the areas where it bears body weight, but a clean mattress may be even more important for your health than a firm one.

Monthly turning, say many modern manufacturers, should be done only when a mattress is new, while it is settling into your body shape, and only occasionally thereafter, but only a mattress that is identical on both sides should be flipped over. If the top layers are different from the bottom ones – as in the "advanced foam" mattresses that mold to your shape with your body warmth – rotation is all that is needed.

A good reason why we need comfortable mattresses: when we are asleep we change our position, on average, four times an hour.

Firm, not overhard, support was the ideal supplied for centuries by horsehair, although the American housewife of 1896 could buy for $11.75 a cotton felt mattress "equal to an $18 mattress of the best hair." From 1901 the luxury mattress had springs set inside. In the most superior types of today, hundreds of springs are sewn into individual pockets, enabling the mattress to support the weights of two individuals without the heavier person making it tilt.

Keeping a mattress clean, especially ridding it of the shed skin and dust mite debris that inevitably build up inside, is probably more important than turning, especially if you suffer from allergies. Light vacuuming – not beating – is the best treatment. If you have a garden, your mattress will benefit from an annual airing in the sun.

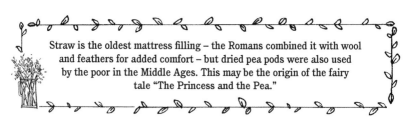

Straw is the oldest mattress filling – the Romans combined it with wool and feathers for added comfort – but dried pea pods were also used by the poor in the Middle Ages. This may be the origin of the fairy tale "The Princess and the Pea."

CLEANLINESS IS NEXT TO GODLINESS

This mantra of the diligent housewife was first declared by John Wesley, the 18th-century founder of Methodism. In the same sermon he also declared neatness of apparel to be "a duty, not a sin."

At the time of John Wesley's pronouncement, cleaning was a daily routine that relied on elbow grease combined with a range of homemade materials including a paste of ashes, sand and grit for scouring, a polish for grates made from bone ash and charcoal, and a beeswax furniture polish. Soap was a luxury reserved for personal use, although surfaces might be scrubbed with lye, an alkali made from ashes. Cleaning was made more difficult by the clutter deemed necessary in the well-appointed middle class home and by the smoke from coal fires.

As to godliness, it is thought that Wesley's saying came originally from an ancient rabbi, Phinehas ben Yair, and for the ancient Jews cleanliness meant much more than the absence of dirt. Washing was a religious ritual for, as it says in the Talmud, "Respect for God demands that the face, the hands and the feet be washed every day." There were – and still are for devout Jews – many sources of uncleanliness, including foods such as pork, shellfish, and the blood of any animal.

This Victorian rhyme about laundry epitomizes the strong connection of the time between dirt and guilt:

They that wash on Monday
Have all the week to dry.
They that wash on Tuesday
Are not so much awry.
They that wash on Wednesday
Are not so much to blame.

They that wash on Thursday
Wash for very shame.
They that wash on Friday
Wash in sorry need.
They that wash on Saturday
Are last sluts indeed.

And of course no one would ever have contemplated doing their washing on a Sunday when they should have been at church!

A BOILED CORK WILL FIT ANY BOTTLE

••

This old tip works because boiling water softens the cork. Although it also makes it swell, the cork becomes malleable enough to be forced into a narrow opening. Modern winemakers soften sterilized corks in a mixture of glycerol and sulfur dioxide before they are rammed home.

The Romans used corks to seal their wine jars, but putting wine in corked bottles has been usual only since the late 17th century, when it was discovered that wine kept and matured much better this way than if left in the barrel. Winemakers of that time also quickly realized that bottles needed to be laid horizontally to prevent the cork from drying out; a dry cork lets in air, which oxidizes the wine and makes it vinegary.

Natural cork comes from the thick, protective bark of the evergreen cork oak (*Quercus suber*), native to the western Mediterranean. It is cultivated particularly in Portugal, which still supplies a large proportion of the market. What makes the cork such an effective stopper is the combination of a honeycomb of minute air cells (over half the volume of cork is empty space) and the waxy, waterproof substance suberin found in its cell walls.

The structure of cork was first seen under the microscope by the English scientist Robert Hooke in the 1660s.

Another old tip for a cork that is a little too large for the bottle is to roll it on the floor and press on it with the sole of a boot or heavy shoe.

The increasing use of the plastic "cork" has as much to do with the incidence of corked wines – wines that are tainted with the chemical trichoroanisole, usually as the result of rotten or mouldy corks – as with the increasing scarcity and expense of the natural material. The screw-top bottle has now become a more convenient and acceptable alternative.

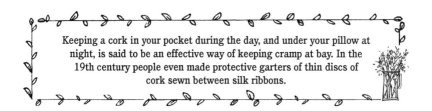

Keeping a cork in your pocket during the day, and under your pillow at night, is said to be an effective way of keeping cramp at bay. In the 19th century people even made protective garters of thin discs of cork sewn between silk ribbons.

NEW BROOMS SWEEP CLEAN

Another way of saying that change is a good thing, but for the housewife it is also a reminder that her cleaning utensils should be renewed regularly.

Appropriately, the broom shares its name with the flexible branches of the plants long used for cleaning (botanically the genera *Cytisus* and *Genista*) for it was these, as well as branches of birch and heather, and tufts of maize, that were probably employed to sweep the floors of early dwellings. Tied together, and with a handle added, bundles of these twigs became the besom.

The wooden broom with bundles of bristles glued into its head dates back to the 15th century, and was still vital to the cleaning repertoire long after the invention of the vacuum cleaner by the London engineer Hubert Cecil Booth in the early 20th century. Brush purchasers of the 1930s were advised to look out for the presence of "inferior mixtures" hidden in a broom. These, it was advised, should be identified "by placing the hand across the surface of the broom and noting the greater readiness with which the bristle will spring back when released, as compared with the less springy substitute."

BROOM MYTHS
Dozens of old sayings relate to the buying and handling of
brooms – apart, of course, from their use as transportation
for both witches and their feline familiars:

- Brooms bought in May sweep the family away.
- If you set a broom in the corner, strangers will come to the house.
- Lay a broom across the doorway to protect the house.
- Throw a broom to ward off witches.
- It is unlucky to put a sweeping brush on a table.
- A servant will not get her wages if the head comes off her
  broom while she is sweeping.

REVIVE CUT FLOWERS BY DIPPING THE STEMS IN HOT WATER

This shock treatment works for flowers with woody stems and some soft-stemmed blooms including dahlias, hellebores and anemones – and for roses limp at the neck. Afterwards, stems need to be left in cold water for a couple of hours before being arranged in a vase.

Flowers go limp because they lack water, often because air bubbles get trapped in their stems. Water at boiling point is recommended for this conditioning treatment; immersion for no more than 30 seconds pushes water quickly up the stems. Ideally, the flower heads and leaves should be loosely wrapped in a clean cloth to prevent them from being damaged by steam. For flowers such as poppies and euphorbias, which exude a milky latex, the recommended heat treatment is not boiling but singeing, to prevent the loss of fluid. Simply hold the cut end of the stalk in a candle or match flame until it is blackened and no more liquid oozes out.

Flower arrangers also use other ruses to help make flowers last longer. These include slitting woody stems and scraping off the bark, and submerging leaves (except grey furry ones) and stems in water for a couple of hours. Putting an aspirin in the vase with cut flowers can prevent wilting, because it has the effect of closing off the stomata, or pores, on the leaf surfaces through which water vapor naturally escapes.

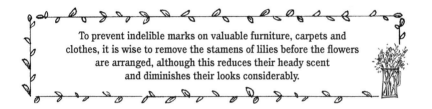

To prevent indelible marks on valuable furniture, carpets and clothes, it is wise to remove the stamens of lilies before the flowers are arranged, although this reduces their heady scent and diminishes their looks considerably.

TACK WELL, SEW BETTER

In dressmaking, and other sorts of sewing, tacking, also known as basting, keeps the fabric in place before seams are stitched together permanently. Accurate tacking is always vital to the fit and finish of any garment, however simple.

After pieces of fabric have been pinned together the best tacking is done by hand, using a thread of contrasting color so that it is easy to see when it is ready to be removed. The ideal way to tack is to knot the thread at one end, and to make long stitches, bringing the needle out each time ¼–½ inch (6–12 mm) beyond the point where it was inserted. For permanent stiffening, dressmakers of the past would tack whalebones into garment seams before the final stitching was done.

Machine sewing then holds fabric pieces firmly in place. The earliest types, like that invented for sewing leather by the Englishman Thomas Saint in 1790, created chain stitches, which easily unraveled if the thread snapped. The breakthrough came with lockstitch, made with one thread above and one below the fabric. The lockstitch machine was invented in 1834 by Walter Hunt, but not patented until 1846 by the Massachusetts mechanic Elias Howe.

It is said that if you break a needle while sewing you should bury it in the ground as a precaution against bad luck.

In 1851 another American, Isaac Singer, made his own version, and although successfully sued by Howe for the patent, subsequently joined forces with him.

Before – and long after – the invention of the sewing machine, hand sewing was a social occupation, as it remains today. Once, women would routinely take their needlework when visiting friends and neighbors and the "sewing bee" existed as much for exchanging practical information, gossip and for storytelling, as for stitching.

CLEAN WALLPAPER WITH STALE BREAD

This old and effective method for fingermarks and light stains can even work on ballpoint marks when fresh. Almost stale – not totally bone dry – bread is best; it will also clean your hands, which is useful if you want to avoid getting them wet.

The cleaning is best done with the inside of the crust, which will not crumble and make a mess. If it doesn't work, a soft pencil eraser may do the trick, but make sure it is spotlessly clean before you start. Modern waterproof wallpapers can be sponged with a barely damp cloth, but if you use detergent, test an area of paper that is well hidden to make sure that the color doesn't come off.

For badly stained paper, try rubbing it with dry, medium oatmeal on a soft cloth.

Timeliness is important too, for as the American Lilian W. Betts advised in *The Art of Housekeeping* of 1896: "The longer the dirt or disfigurement remains, the more difficult it is to remove." She also had sound advice on mending torn wallpaper, which still holds good: "Never put the patch on with a straight edge... Cut the edge in uneven scallops and points to match the figures [of the pattern] perfectly. Sometimes it will be almost impossible to discover the patch on the walls."

Wallpaper evolved as a substitute for the thick wall hangings that decorated and helped to insulate homes up to the 19th century. Early papers of the late 17th and early 18th centuries were small, simple block-printed sheets, rather like tiles. Elaborate flocked designs, imitations of Italian silk velvet, were particularly desirable in grand Georgian homes, but wallpaper did not become affordable or popular until the 1840s, when it was first machine printed in two colors, using a technique adapted from calico printing.

DON'T STORE BISCUITS IN THE CAKE TIN

Moistness from any kind of cake will quickly make crisp biscuits, cookies and crackers go soft and soggy. The prudent housekeeper keeps biscuits and cakes in separate, airtight tins to guarantee their individual freshness and keeping qualities.

First, the terms. In Britain a biscuit is a snappy Rich Tea or Digestive, but in the USA it is something softer, similar to an English scone. The American cookie is the nearest equivalent to the British biscuit. In northeast Scotland "soft biscuits" are buns made from bread dough with butter and sugar added. The word *biscuit* comes from the Latin *panis biscotus*, which means "bread twice cooked." Biscuits belong, as Mrs. Beeton says, to "the class of unfermented bread and are, perhaps, the most wholesome of that class."

The simnel was originally a biscuit, not the fruit and marzipan cake we now associate with Easter. It was made from sweet dough that was first boiled, then oven baked.

Biscuits are not necessarily cooked in the oven. From the Middle Ages onwards, wafers were made by heating a thin layer of mixture on a heated plate, and even before that the Romans made deep-fried biscuits from what was essentially a sweetened pasta dough.

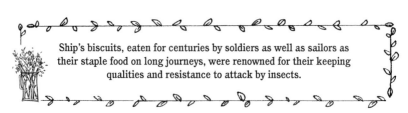

Ship's biscuits, eaten for centuries by soldiers as well as sailors as their staple food on long journeys, were renowned for their keeping qualities and resistance to attack by insects.

FIT A CANDLE TO A CANDLESTICK: DIP IT IN HOT WATER

The simplest and easiest way to soften the wax and allow a good fit, it is also safer and more reliable than trying to melt the candle end with a lighted match or the flame of a cigarette lighter.

Soft candlelight provides a subtle evening ambience, but is no longer a necessity in the home. If a candle burns blue it is said that a spirit has entered the house.

The first candles were made by immersing rushes or flax fibers in animal or fish fat (tallow) or in beeswax. Even by the 1920s, when most towns and cities were lit by electric light, country housewives still saved their kitchen "scummings" for making tallow candles, which though economical gave out a yellow light and an acrid smell.

Candles improve with keeping. Left exposed to the air for a few months the wax hardens and will burn longer and brighter.

Most candles are now made from paraffin wax and machine molded. The best are made from spermaceti, the waxy substance found inside the head of the sperm whale.

A British Act of Parliament of 1860 defined a "standard candle" as one made of spermaceti wax, six of which together weighed 1 pound (450 g), and which burnt 120 grains of wax an hour. From this specification came the original measures of gas and electric light in terms of candle power.

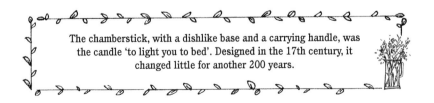

The chamberstick, with a dishlike base and a carrying handle, was the candle 'to light you to bed'. Designed in the 17th century, it changed little for another 200 years.

REMOVE WATERMARKS FROM FURNITURE WITH MAYONNAISE

This can work on light marks by drawing the water out of the wood, but is by no means infallible even if, as some experts recommend, you mix in a little cigarette ash or toothpaste.

Even if this method proves effective – and you need to rub the affected area gently for half an hour or more so that the oil in the mayonnaise can work into the wood, or leave the mixture in place for 12 hours before buffing – you may still have a problem. Because both ash and toothpaste are abrasive they can ruin the piece's finish. A final, thorough waxing may help, but the bottom line is that water in any form, including wine, is bad for polished wood and a valuable piece may need professional restoration.

To prevent problems, protect your table with coasters. These were invented in the 1760s to avoid wine spillages on furniture and linens and were originally made from silver or Old Sheffield plate. They were not flat like modern coasters, but like shallow dishes, initially quite plain but by the early Victorian period intricately decorated. Coasters got their name from the (male-only) after-dinner custom of rolling back the tablecloth and coasting – sliding – the port, placed in its smooth-bottomed container, from drinker to drinker.

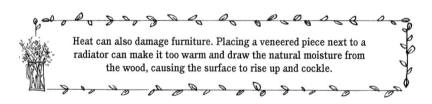

Heat can also damage furniture. Placing a veneered piece next to a radiator can make it too warm and draw the natural moisture from the wood, causing the surface to rise up and cockle.

DON'T FORGET TO DUST YOUR HOUSEPLANTS

Dust is not only unsightly but clogs the stomata, or pores, in the leaves through which plants "breathe." But plants in modern homes fare better than those in stuffy Victorian parlors.

When treating indoor plants, use a clean cloth and wipe large, glossy leaves individually; more feathery leaves are best sprayed with water. Don't waste money on proprietary cleaners; if used too frequently they can also clog the pores.

The need for houseplant cleaning reached its height in the Victorian period, when plants such as the aspidistra – nicknamed the cast iron plant for its sturdy resistance – were grown in living rooms thick with smoke from gaslights and open fires, and dust from heavy hangings and furniture coverings.

After a death in the family, an old custom was to tie lengths of black crêpe (a type of crinkled silk) around indoor plants to prevent them dying too.

To protect them from pollution, 19th-century householders would grow ferns, which were all the rage, enclosed in glass Wardian cases. These were effectively miniature greenhouses, containing their own self-sustaining microclimate. They had been invented by the London doctor and ardent naturalist Dr. Nathaniel Bagshaw Ward. In 1833 he filled one of them with ferns, grasses and flowering plants; it subsequently survived the journey from Britain to Australia. On the return journey, Australian specimens filled the case and arrived "in the most healthy and vigorous condition."

TIPS TO KEEP HOUSEPLANTS ALIVE
- Don't overwater plants, especially in winter.
- Let the compost dry out between waterings.
- Deadhead faded flowers.
- Remove dead or yellowing leaves.
- Feed plants in their growing season, usually spring to autumn.
- Avoid wetting the furry leaves of African violets.

TO GET YOUR WASHING WHITE, DRY IT IN THE SUN

Oxygen and ozone in the air work as bleaches that not only whiten but disinfect the wash – not to mention the added benefit of the wonderfully fresh aroma of sundried linens. On the downside, washing left outside is at the mercy of the weather.

If there is a light breeze, hanging the washing outdoors can also help remove creases from clothes and cut down on ironing. However thick items like towels can get hard and stiff when dried in the sun, and may be better finished off in a tumble dryer or airing cupboard.

There is an art to hanging out the washing. First you need to choose what to pin out: woolens, silks and delicate fabrics are better kept indoors and dried flat. It would have been second nature to the laundry maid to peg socks by the toes, shirts by the tails and dresses by the shoulders. Adjacent tea towels and handkerchiefs she would have pegged together at the corners, making a neat, firm row on the washing line.

For securing items such as sheets and jeans so that they don't blow away there is still nothing to beat the traditional push-on American peg, or clothespin, made from a single piece of wood. This is not only durable but, unlike the spring-grip peg (which comes in plastic as well as wood and is most suitable for more delicate items), has no metal to rust. The

> *In seafaring communities, wives will never wash clothes on the day their menfolk set sail, for fear that this will wash their ships away.*

gypsy peg, rarely seen nowadays, is made from two pieces of whittled wood held together at one end with a band of metal.

CLEAN BOTTLES WITH EGGSHELLS

When marks are inaccessible with a brush, crushed eggshells shaken inside a bottle or decanter with warm water and a little washing-up liquid make an excellent and effective cleaner.

Alternatively, you can buy boxes of "magic" metal balls that do the same job by abrading the inside of the bottle. These are the modern version of the lead shot that butlers traditionally used in decanters, with the addition of brandy. Coal ashes shaken with hot or cold water are another old-fashioned cleaner.

Eggshells have other good uses. Crushed and spread in the garden they can help to keep slugs off your most vulnerable plants. In the kitchen they can be used to clarify consommés; the cloudy particles in the liquid cling to the eggshells, which can then be filtered out.

> *Since the 18th century wine bottles have been molded into identifiable shapes for specific wine regions and grapes, from the "shouldered" Bordeaux bottle to the squat, round one for Chianti.*

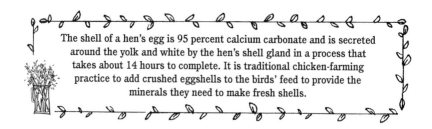

The shell of a hen's egg is 95 percent calcium carbonate and is secreted around the yolk and white by the hen's shell gland in a process that takes about 14 hours to complete. It is traditional chicken-farming practice to add crushed eggshells to the birds' feed to provide the minerals they need to make fresh shells.

PUT WHITE WINE ON A RED WINE STAIN

Red wine on a pale carpet or favorite sweater is the accident everyone dreads, but white wine is better drunk than wasted on a stain! Salt may work to a degree (and is good for bloodstains) but a mild detergent is by far the best remedy.

When poured on to a stain, the bubbles in soda water can help to lift a red wine stain from carpet or fabric fibers, but whatever remedy you choose, haste and a gentle touch are essential. Your aim should be to prevent the stain from "setting," spreading or being rubbed into the fibers. The advantage of the detergent approach is that you can whiz up a foam that can be palmed on to a

To remove wine stains from linen, common 19th-century advice was to hold it in milk "while boiling on the fire."

carpet to work on the stain without getting the pile soaking wet. The residue can then be carefully removed with a clean cloth, without rubbing, and the area neutralized with a dilute solution of white (not wine or malt) vinegar.

OTHER GOOD TIPS FOR SPILLS AND STAINS

Coffee and tea – detergent followed by vinegar, as for red wine.

Chewing gum – put a bag of ice cubes on the offending area, or put a garment in the freezer for at least an hour, then scrape off the hardened gum.

Ink, oil-based paint, butter – commercial dry cleaning fluid, followed by diluted household ammonia.

Blood, egg, milk, chocolate – detergent in cold water (to avoid cooking the stain), then vinegar diluted in water.

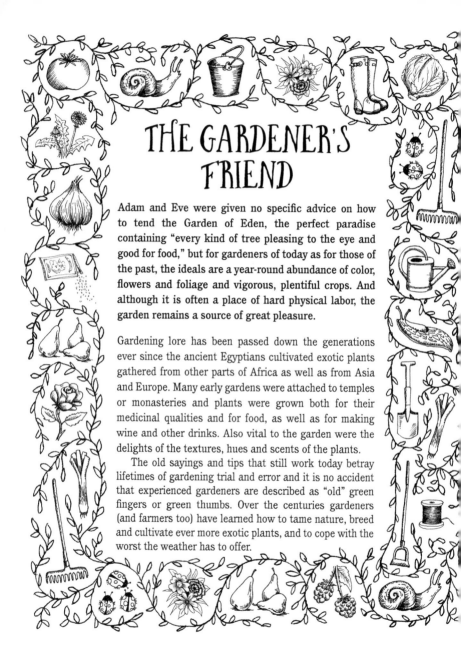

THE GARDENER'S FRIEND

Adam and Eve were given no specific advice on how to tend the Garden of Eden, the perfect paradise containing "every kind of tree pleasing to the eye and good for food," but for gardeners of today as for those of the past, the ideals are a year-round abundance of color, flowers and foliage and vigorous, plentiful crops. And although it is often a place of hard physical labor, the garden remains a source of great pleasure.

Gardening lore has been passed down the generations ever since the ancient Egyptians cultivated exotic plants gathered from other parts of Africa as well as from Asia and Europe. Many early gardens were attached to temples or monasteries and plants were grown both for their medicinal qualities and for food, as well as for making wine and other drinks. Also vital to the garden were the delights of the textures, hues and scents of the plants.

The old sayings and tips that still work today betray lifetimes of gardening trial and error and it is no accident that experienced gardeners are described as "old" green fingers or green thumbs. Over the centuries gardeners (and farmers too) have learned how to tame nature, breed and cultivate ever more exotic plants, and to cope with the worst the weather has to offer.

DON'T USE TAP WATER ON AZALEAS

The key to this reliable piece of advice is that azaleas are acid lovers. Most tap water contains enough lime to make it alkaline and so endanger the health of these loveliest of spring blooms.

Azaleas are not a genus in their own right but a type of rhododendron, with orange, yellow, pink or white flowers and deciduous or evergreen foliage. First in cultivation were the deciduous Ghent azaleas, bred from 1815 from seeds of *Rhododendron arboretum* gathered in Nepal and sent to the West (packed in tins of brown sugar at the Calcutta Botanical Garden) by Nathaniel Wallich, the garden's director.

The famous Victorian gardener William Robinson maintained that that "there is nothing more charming in the garden than the table-like tiers of azalea flowers."

What azaleas like most of all is rainwater, which in cities may even be slightly acid because carbon dioxide in the air dissolves in moisture in the atmosphere to make a very diluted solution of carbonic acid. If you have no way of collecting rainwater for an azalea growing in a pot indoors, boiled and cooled water is a good alternative.

Azaleas grow best in a woodland setting as they prefer light shade and soil that does not dry out but drains well. They need plenty of humus and will appreciate an annual feed in early spring with one of the specially formulated soil enrichers available for acid-loving plants. If you adore azaleas but don't have acid soil, then grow them in large pots filled with peat or peat-free substitute, mixed with leaf mold, garden soil or medium coarse grit.

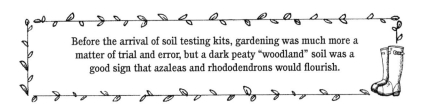

Before the arrival of soil testing kits, gardening was much more a matter of trial and error, but a dark peaty "woodland" soil was a good sign that azaleas and rhododendrons would flourish.

SOW BROAD BEANS ON BOXING DAY

A catchy way of saying that broad beans (*Vicia faba*) can be successfully overwintered, although both modern seed producers and their predecessors recommend sowing in mid to late autumn while the soil is still warm. The earlier they are sown the less prone the young plants will be, it is said, to attack by blackfly.

Gardeners can choose between two types of broad beans: short-podded Windsor beans (probably the original ingredient of brown Windsor soup), with four large beans to a pod, and longpod varieties with up to eight beans per pod. To stop seeds being eaten by mice, 19th-century gardeners would roll the seeds in paraffin before planting.

Large beans with tough skins are better dried, and these are the key ingredient of the ancient Egyptian dish ful medames, one of the first cooked dishes ever recorded and still eaten today.

Eating broad beans has long been associated with the mysterious, sudden onset of a rare but debilitating illness, and modern medicine has revealed the beans to be responsible for setting off attacks of favism, typified by headaches, blurred vision, dizziness and nausea – symptoms that come on within an hour or two of consumption. It is a hereditary condition, caused by the lack of an enzyme essential to broad bean digestion, and resulting in the rapid destruction of red blood cells.

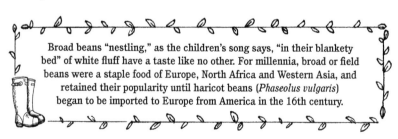

Broad beans "nestling," as the children's song says, "in their blankety bed" of white fluff have a taste like no other. For millennia, broad or field beans were a staple food of Europe, North Africa and Western Asia, and retained their popularity until haricot beans (*Phaseolus vulgaris*) began to be imported to Europe from America in the 16th century.

NEVER MOVE A PEONY

A peony will last a lifetime as long as you resist the temptation to move it from one bed to another. Move one if you must – there is a chance that it may survive. The tubers from which peonies grow are prized in legend for their healing powers, but it is said that uprooting a peony will bring the worst of ill fortune.

Named after the Greek physician Paeon, peonies (*Paeonia* spp) have been cultivated since at least the 7th century, when the Chinese grew them for both their medicinal properties and their beauty. Today's gardener can choose from a huge range of species and varieties, from the sumptuous, ruffled double pink *P. lactiflora* "Sarah Bernhardt" to *P. mlokosewitchii*, known colloquially as "Molly the Witch," whose soft bluish-green foliage is topped with single lemon yellow flowers.

A Mr. Parkinson, writing in Theatrum Botanicum *in 1640 on cures for epilepsy, says: "I saw a child freed from that disease, that had for eight whole months together, worn a good piece of the [peony] root about him."*

Peonies need a fertile, well-composted soil and plenty of sunshine, although they are prone to damage by spring frosts if iced leaves are quickly warmed by bright sunshine. They arrived in Britain in profusion in the 1880s and the numerous hybrids that were cultivated reached the height of fashion in Edwardian times.

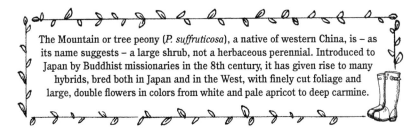

The Mountain or tree peony (*P. suffruticosa*), a native of western China, is – as its name suggests – a large shrub, not a herbaceous perennial. Introduced to Japan by Buddhist missionaries in the 8th century, it has given rise to many hybrids, bred both in Japan and in the West, with finely cut foliage and large, double flowers in colors from white and pale apricot to deep carmine.

PLANT CLEMATIS WITH THEIR HEADS IN THE SUN AND THEIR ROOTS IN THE SHADE

Although they love the sun, and will thrive on a south-facing wall, clematis certainly prefer shade around their roots. These garden favorites now come in so many varieties that it is possible to have one in bloom in every season of the year.

All clematis appreciate careful planting, with the base of the stem about 6 inches (15 cm) below the soil surface to encourage more shoots to emerge from below ground. Give them a cool root run by siting them in the shade of other plants. Fatal to clematis is wilt, a fungus that rots the stems. Its threat is greatest in the first two years, before plants have grown wilt-resistant woody stems, and to early flowering varieties. Hot, humid weather makes plants especially vulnerable. The only possible cure is to cut away all diseased stems, water in a fungicide and feed the plant well to encourage new growth.

Wild clematis, Clematis vitalba, *is called traveler's joy or old man's beard for the white, fluffy seed heads that appear in late autumn and last all winter. It grows in particular profusion along the Pilgrim's Way that joins London and Canterbury.*

FOR PRUNING CLEMATIS USE THIS HANDY RULE OF THUMB
If a clematis flowers early – cut it back immediately after flowering.
If it flowers in mid season – wait to prune until early spring, and do not be severe.
If it flowers late in the year – prune in early spring, but cut the stems to about 1 feet (30 cm) from the ground.

PROTECT NEWLY SOWN GRASS SEED WITH BLACK COTTON THREAD

With the addition of "rag flutterers and rattles of tin and glass," as one 19th-century manual recommends, this is the tried and trusted way of scaring birds away from a lawn in the making, though not as quick and easy to put in place as today's birdproof netting or fleece.

The first lawns were probably medieval pleasure gardens planted with sweet-smelling herbs, but it was the Tudor love of ball games that gave birth to the quintessentially English lawn, which took shape from the greens and bowling alleys of the 16th century. Early lawns included daisies, violets and speedwell in profusion and only from the 18th century did the perfect greensward become the only acceptable foil for beds of flowers and shrubs.

Except for perfectionists, lawn rolling has become confined to sports grounds, but in 1863 the Journal of Horticulture *advised that "mowing alone will not secure a good bottom without that compression which the roller...tends to give."*

For the domestic garden, the Victorians favored seeding over turfing, which gave patchy results at best. As now, all-purpose seed mixtures containing species such as rye grass (*Lolium perenne*), sheep's fescue (*Festuca ovina*) and meadow grass (*Poa pratensis*) were planted, but the lawn would also have contained clovers and trefoils. Pre-preparation was – and is – all-important, and could take a whole year to complete.

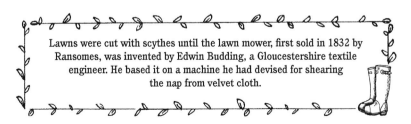

Lawns were cut with scythes until the lawn mower, first sold in 1832 by Ransomes, was invented by Edwin Budding, a Gloucestershire textile engineer. He based it on a machine he had devised for shearing the nap from velvet cloth.

KILL DANDELIONS WITH SALT

Salt is a good old-fashioned organic weedkiller that works by interfering with the natural functioning of plant cells, or by preventing their growth, but it is not as effective as modern chemical treatments.

To kill dandelions in a lawn, old gardening books recommended digging out the offending plant, then dropping a little salt into the hole to kill off any remains of the root and so prevent the weed springing up again in the same place. Another reliable but drastic method was to dip an iron skewer in sulfuric acid and force it into the heart of the plant.

The dandelion's common name is a corruption of the French **dent de lion**, *meaning lion's tooth, and probably refers to the toothed leaves.*

Modern weedkillers for zapping perennial troublemakers like dandelions contain chemicals such as glyphosate and can be applied as "spot" treatment on individual plants. For lawns, try a "weed and feed" mixture, but be sure to apply it after heavy rain, or when the lawn has been well watered, or it will scorch the grass.

Dandelions (*Taraxacum officinale*) were once cultivated as salad greens. Gardeners were advised to lift the roots in autumn, place them in boxes of soil and force them into growth in a warm, dark place. The foliage has a slightly bitter taste not unlike chicory.

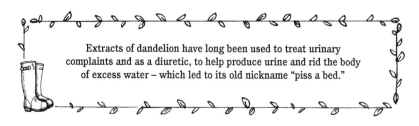

Extracts of dandelion have long been used to treat urinary complaints and as a diuretic, to help produce urine and rid the body of excess water – which led to its old nickname "piss a bed."

TO KEEP HYDRANGEAS PINK, SPRINKLE THE SOIL WITH LIME

Pink is the natural color of hydrangeas, but to keep them that way you need to make sure that the soil stays alkaline – which is why lime does the trick so effectively.

Hydrangea flowers – nicknamed "changeables" by the Victorians – are nature's soil indicators but are exact opposites to litmus paper. On acid soils the blooms will turn blue, but you can alter their color artificially from pink to blue by adding aluminium sulfate to the soil or watering them with a bluing agent. Rusty nails or copper wire planted near the roots are effective old-fashioned bluing treatments.

Hydrangeas get their name from the shape of their seed pods, which look like drinking cups. In Greek hydor *means water and* aggeion, *vessel.*

The flowers on a hydrangea head are of two kinds, the small fertile flowers and the showy sterile flowers, called ray florets. The mop-headed hortensias and the flat-headed lacecaps of *Hydrangea macrophylla* are the best-known sorts, but they like a protected position in the garden. *H. paniculata* "Grandiflora" is a hardier choice for cold areas. For a more unusual look, search out elegant *H. aspera*, with soft felted leaves and large heads of fertile flowers bordered by just a few ray florets.

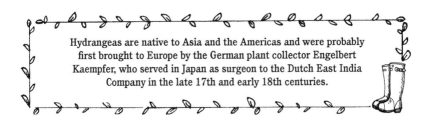

Hydrangeas are native to Asia and the Americas and were probably first brought to Europe by the German plant collector Engelbert Kaempfer, who served in Japan as surgeon to the Dutch East India Company in the late 17th and early 18th centuries.

PLANT MARIGOLDS TO KEEP WHITEFLY AWAY

French marigolds (*Tagetes patula*) are the best deterrents, although unlikely to be totally effective. They work best in a confined space, such as a greenhouse, where they can be used to protect tomatoes and chrysanthemums, and they should be planted tight up to vulnerable plants.

It is probably the musty odor of French marigold flowers that deters whitefly, although their color may also attract the insects away from crop plants. Playing to this color preference, try hanging yellow sticky flypapers in the greenhouse or above plants growing outdoors. The whitefly, which look like tiny moths, will come to a permanent halt as they adhere to the trap.

Another good organic control is the parasitic wasp *Encarsia formosa*, which works by laying its eggs in the whitefly larvae. The grubs that emerge from the eggs devour their hosts, preventing them from hatching into adult flies.

Outdoors, plants most prone to whitefly are brassicas of all kinds, including cabbages, cauliflowers and broccoli. Infestation can be so bad that the leaves become covered with a sticky black substance and clouds of insects fly up when the plants are touched. Chemical controls that work best are those based on pyrethrum, sprayed regularly on the undersides of the leaves, or a systemic insecticide.

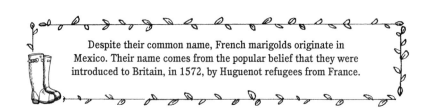

Despite their common name, French marigolds originate in Mexico. Their name comes from the popular belief that they were introduced to Britain, in 1572, by Huguenot refugees from France.

TO HELP GERMINATE PARSLEY SEEDS, POUR ON BOILING WATER

You can do this after the seeds have been planted to help speed the notoriously slow germination of this garden herb, which can take up to 70 or even 90 days to appear. In the parsley bed – as well as under the gooseberry bush – is the place babies are said to come from.

Another good tip for parsley is to soak the seeds in warm water before they are put into the ground. You can also start seeds off indoors and transplant the seedlings later, although many people think that this is unlucky, and possibly even an omen of death. As to variety, the cook's choice is the taller flat-leaved or "continental"

> *"Where parsley grows faster," say the superstitious, "the mistress is master." In other words, the woman of the house rules the roost. The plant is also said to grow better when seeds are planted by a woman, not a man.*

type, also known as French parsley, or by its botanical name *Petroselinum crispum* var. *neapolitanum*. It habitually has more flavor than "Moss Curled" and other curly-leaved cultivars.

Parsley can be found growing wild in southern Europe. Although the Romans gathered and used it they probably did not use it in the kitchen; they planted parsley deliberately only on graves, hence its association with ill fortune. Parsley reached British gardens and tables in the mid 16th century, although it was especially commended for flavor by the Emperor Charlemagne some 800 years before it crossed the English Channel.

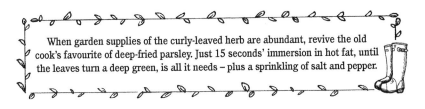

When garden supplies of the curly-leaved herb are abundant, revive the old cook's favourite of deep-fried parsley. Just 15 seconds' immersion in hot fat, until the leaves turn a deep green, is all it needs – plus a sprinkling of salt and pepper.

NEVER PLANT CABBAGES IN THE SAME PLACE TWO YEARS RUNNING

••

Or any other brassicas – broccoli, cauliflowers or Brussels sprouts – for that matter. One of the good reasons for rotating garden crops is to help keep diseases at bay including, for brassicas, debilitating club root.

Club root lives up to its name, swelling and distorting the roots of plants. This fungal disease, also called "finger and toe," strikes during the growing season and severely hampers leaf production, resulting in leaves that are yellow and sickly, although perfectly edible. There is no treatment other than to burn affected plants. The best prevention is to treat the soil before planting with about 8 ounces (227 g) hydrated lime per square yard (240 g/sq m). The calcium in the lime is thought to deter fungal spores from germinating and penetrating the roots.

The Romans ate large amounts of cabbage as a health food. And the latest research suggests that it may help to keep cancer at bay, especially cancer of the colon.

The theory behind the rotation of crops goes back to the three-field strip system of medieval farming. Each year one of the three fields was left unplanted (fallow) to allow it to recover its fertility. Good composting and manuring makes a fallow period unnecessary in the average garden but good drainage, especially of clay soils, will always help vegetable health.

IMPROVE THE SOIL BY DIGGING IN NEWSPAPERS

A good, eco-friendly low-cost ruse for adding "structure" to light, chalky or sandy soil, although you will also need to add plenty of compost to boost soil nutrients. Water-absorbent low-quality paper (whatever the editorial style) rots down fastest.

The problem on fine soils is that the water drains from them too quickly, leaving plant roots dehydrated and leaching out nutrients. Apart from newspapers, which need to be finely shredded to speed rotting (there is no evidence that the ink has any ill effects on plants), try adding beached seaweed, if you can get it legally and are sure that it is uncontaminated. Well washed to rid it of salt, which is lethal to plants in large quantities,

That clay bakes hard in the sun – and even harder when heated in a fire – is the logic behind pottery making, a craft with a history of at least 25,000 years.

seaweed rots quickly and adds potassium and iodine. On light soils, the sticky alginates it contains help bind soil particles together.

Clay soils have the opposite problem. Their fine particles stick together tightly, making them rock hard when dry so that they impede drainage. For these, shredded paper plus grit, sharp sand (not builder's sand, which is too fine and likely to be full of lime), fine gravel or pea shingle all work well as improvers. They need to be added at about 1½ spade depths, with a layer of well-rotted manure placed on top.

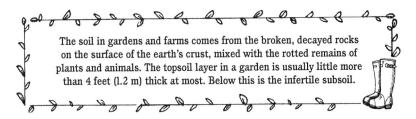

The soil in gardens and farms comes from the broken, decayed rocks on the surface of the earth's crust, mixed with the rotted remains of plants and animals. The topsoil layer in a garden is usually little more than 4 feet (1.2 m) thick at most. Below this is the infertile subsoil.

DETER SLUGS WITH GRAVEL

Every gardener has a favorite method of dealing with slugs and snails – from the chemical blast of pellets to wildlife-friendly methods such as surrounding plants with gravel to impede the pests' progress.

Since slugs and snails can ravage beautiful young hostas, delphiniums or clematis overnight, not to mention destroying lettuces and other salad plants, and even climbing up raspberry canes to gorge on ripe fruit, it is hardly surprising that gardeners not only loathe them with a passion but are forever searching for good methods of deterring or killing them. Some people swear that the only way to get rid of slugs and snails is to go out into the garden at night with a torch and pick them individually off the plants – and they do just that.

A "slugabed" is an Old English word for a lazy lie-abed. But a slughorn is a battle trumpet.

Slugs and snails are mollusks whose bodies consist largely of a muscular foot (which in snails curls up inside the shell when they are inactive or threatened). This not only secretes their tell-tale lubricating silvery trails, but contains organs of touch and smell powerful enough to detect potential food from a distance. Once a tasty vegetable meal has been located the creatures munch through it systematically using their sharp, file-like oral rasps.

Many suppliers advertise hostas that they claim are bred to have some resistance to slugs, with variety names that include "Big Daddy," "Invincible" and "Great Expectations," but they are unlikely to be able to stave off attacks completely. The alternative solution is to choose plants that won't be eaten; for example, slugs really don't like the furry foliage of plants such as stachys.

NATURAL SLUG REPELLENTS

Choose from some of these organic methods of slug control that avoid the use of pellets:

Gravel and glass chippings – uncomfortable and difficult for slugs to negotiate.

Beer traps – death by drowning; the beer smell is irresistible.

Copper rings – offensive to the taste buds on slugs' bodies.

Diluted cat urine – interferes with the body chemistry of mollusks.

Coffee grounds – caffeine poisoning is fatal to slugs.

Crushed garlic – probably damages their nervous system.

Frogs, toads and hedgehogs – dine on slugs and snails.

Upturned grapefruit halves with holes cut in them – the creatures glide in then can't escape.

A WET SUMMER BRINGS ON TOMATO BLIGHT

The fungi that devastate an outdoor tomato crop flourish most in wet weather, and the warmer it is the worse the problem. What's more, the spores linger in the soil from year to year, making blight notoriously hard to eradicate.

A tomato plant infested with blight is a sorry sight. Blackened leaves hang limply from its weakened stem, while those fruits not already rotting on the ground below are brown or blackened with the fungus. The only thing to do is to collect all the infected material and either burn it or dispose of it with general household waste. Because the spores do not rot it should never be put in the compost heap or green waste recycling bin.

The tomato was greeted with great suspicion when it first arrived in Europe, possibly because of its resemblance to the red berries of its poisonous relative the woody (often wrongly called deadly) nightshade (Solanum dulcamara).

Blight is as hard to prevent as it is to eradicate. Fortnightly spraying with Bordeaux mixture (made from copper sulfate and hydrated lime) may work before and during attacks, but is far from foolproof. Growing your tomatoes indoors or on a patio is the best way to avoid blight. Worst of all is to cultivate them on an allotment where spores blow readily from plot to plot.

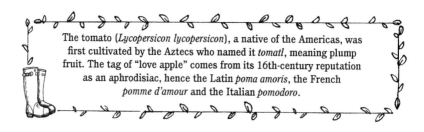

The tomato (*Lycopersicon lycopersicon*), a native of the Americas, was first cultivated by the Aztecs who named it *tomatl*, meaning plump fruit. The tag of "love apple" comes from its 16th-century reputation as an aphrodisiac, hence the Latin *poma amoris*, the French *pomme d'amour* and the Italian *pomodoro*.

LADYBIRDS ARE THE GARDENERS' FRIENDS

The ladybird or ladybug is our ally because both adults and larvae, also known as "garden crocodiles," are voracious devourers of both aphids and the scale insects that attack garden flowers and crops.

Ladybirds (members of the insect family Coccinellidae) are small winged, spotted beetles, usually colored in a combination of either red or yellow with black. An individual can eat up to 150 aphids in a day. The eggs, mostly laid on the undersides of leaves, hatch into elongated larvae, dark gray with colored blotches. These consume many times their own weight in other insects and their eggs. After shedding their external "skin" several times they turn into the spherical pupae from which adults hatch.

The most common European ladybird is the red seven-spot Coccinella 7-punctata. The yellow Thea 22-punctata has 22 black spots, as its name suggests.

The ladybird or "beetle of our lady" got its name from its dedication to the Virgin Mary in the Middle Ages. The children's rhyme "Ladybird, ladybird fly away home/Your house is on fire and your children will burn" is said to come from the burning of the hop fields in England at the end of the harvest, which destroyed many of these insects. But as well as flying away when disturbed, ladybirds will lie on their backs and "play possum." To make themselves unappetizing to bird predators they also exude blobs of pungent yellow "blood."

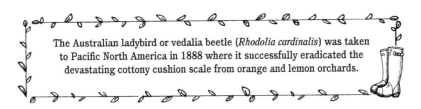

The Australian ladybird or vedalia beetle (*Rhodolia cardinalis*) was taken to Pacific North America in 1888 where it successfully eradicated the devastating cottony cushion scale from orange and lemon orchards.

STOP PICKING ASPARAGUS ON THE LONGEST DAY

• •

The logic behind this good advice is to give the asparagus plants plenty of time to renew their underground resources before the onset of winter. Quite by chance, the longest day of the year coincides with the traditional end of the six-week cropping season for English asparagus.

Asparagus is easy to grow as long as you have the patience to wait for the crowns to mature, since even if you plant three-year-old crowns (roots) the spears should not be cut for two years. But given good drainage, fertile soil and an annual top dressing of compost, a healthy bed can last for two decades and more. Growers of the past would bury animal horns, especially those of sheep, to help keep their asparagus beds fertile.

The asparagus plant is a kind of lily, probably cultivated since ancient Egyptian times. It was a favorite of the ancient Romans and Pliny the Elder described asparagus grown in Ravenna as so large as to be "three to the pound." Although it makes no difference to the crop, male and female flowers are borne on different plants. Choosing all male plants will stop the spread of the seedlings that can sprout in profusion from shed female berries.

The American guru Emily Post recommends in *Etiquette* (1960) that although "'by reputation this is a finger food…the ungraceful appearance of a bent stalk of asparagus falling limply into someone's mouth and the fact that moisture is also likely to drip from the end have been the reasons that most fastidious people invariably eat it – at least in part – with the fork."

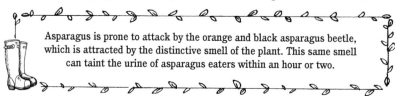

Asparagus is prone to attack by the orange and black asparagus beetle, which is attracted by the distinctive smell of the plant. This same smell can taint the urine of asparagus eaters within an hour or two.

IF YOUR WEEDS ARE NETTLES, YOUR SOIL IS RICH IN NITROGEN

True. Nettles and many other weeds are excellent indicators of the soil type you have in your garden, the improvement it needs and the flowers, shrubs and trees that will thrive in it.

Since nettles mean nitrogen, they are a sign that your plot will be ideal for leafy vegetables like spinach that also need nitrogen to thrive, but may be less suitable for fruit trees because it can stimulate them to make too much leaf and too little blossom (and fruit). To balance up the soil treat it with potash, which on soil already rich in nitrogen is best supplied as potassium sulfate.

The young leaves of nettles have long been used to make an iron-rich herbal tea but they should be picked before May Day. After that, so legend has it, the Devil uses them to make his shirts.

Phosphorus is the other essential element for fertility, ensuring good root and fruit formation. It is best applied to the soil as phosphates, either in quick-acting liquid form or as slow-release rock phosphate. Good organic sources are farmyard manure and bonemeal.

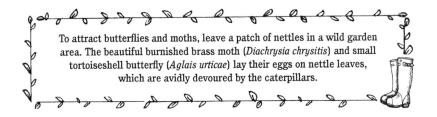

To attract butterflies and moths, leave a patch of nettles in a wild garden area. The beautiful burnished brass moth (*Diachrysia chrysitis*) and small tortoiseshell butterfly (*Aglais urticae*) lay their eggs on nettle leaves, which are avidly devoured by the caterpillars.

SOIL SIGNS

Look out for all of these good soil indicators:

Nitrogen rich – stinging nettles (*Urtica dioica*),
black nightshade (*Solanum nigrum*).
Lime rich – bindweed (*Convolvulus arvensis*).
Lime deficient – chamomile (*Chamaemelum nobile*).
Loam – tansy (*Tanacetum vulgare*), dandelions (*Taraxacum* spp).
Clay – coltsfoot *(Tussilago farfara).*

BEANS AND PEAS NOURISH THE SOIL

This is true up to a point but these crops, which have long associations
with good fortune, also feed hungrily from the soil throughout their
growing season.

Beans, peas and other leguminous plants have earned their soil-improving
reputation from the fact that they can "fix" nitrogen from the air and
use it to help their growth. They do this
by virtue of the small white nodules
on their roots. These are packed with
nitrogen-grabbing bacteria of the genus
Rhizobium that "infect" the roots of the
young plants, making them – and their
decorative relatives such as lupins and

*French beans get their name
from the country where they
are traditionally most popular,
although in fact they are native to
South America, probably Peru.*

brooms – able to thrive on soil that is low in nitrogen.

Despite their ability to make use of nitrogen from the air – they rarely
suffer from the leaf-yellowing typical of nitrogen deficiency – beans and
peas also need plenty of phosphorus and potassium, the two essential

elements represented respectively by the chemical symbols P and K in an NPK fertilizer. They are easily supplied in well-rotted compost and other organic mixtures such as blood and bonemeal. For tenderness, legumes also like good drainage for, as the old saying goes, "Sow beans in mud and they'll grow like wood."

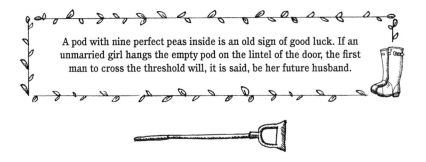

A pod with nine perfect peas inside is an old sign of good luck. If an unmarried girl hangs the empty pod on the lintel of the door, the first man to cross the threshold will, it is said, be her future husband.

DON'T PICK BRUSSELS SPROUTS UNTIL THEY'VE HAD A FROST ON THEM

This is a neat way of saying that most maincrop varieties of this winter vegetable won't be ready to pick until late autumn after the first frosts, although it is possible to plant earlier croppers. However, very cold weather makes even the hardiest varieties mushy and inedible when they thaw out.

Brussels sprouts (*Brassica oleracea*) are not difficult to grow as long as you have fertile, well-manured soil, ideally improved with lime, and enough space to accommodate them. Plants need to be set at least 2 feet (60 cm) apart in each direction and placed firmly in the soil in spring to prevent root sway. They also need protection from marauding pigeons; fine netting has the added advantage of deterring cabbage white butterflies from laying their eggs on the leaves, which later hatch into hungry caterpillars.

For a good all-purpose variety choose an F1 hybrid such as "Breeze," which has smooth, dark green buttons and is a vigorous grower. Of the early hybrids "Peer Gynt" is a reliable selection. For sprouts with a difference grow a red variety such as "Red Bull," whose color intensifies as the weather grows colder.

It is assumed (though not known for certain) that Brussels sprouts originated in Belgium as a rather odd kind of cabbage with miniatures growing up its stem. The first reliable references to sprouts in English and French cooking are from the 18th century, while in the USA Thomas Jefferson definitely planted them in his garden at Monticello in Virginia in 1812.

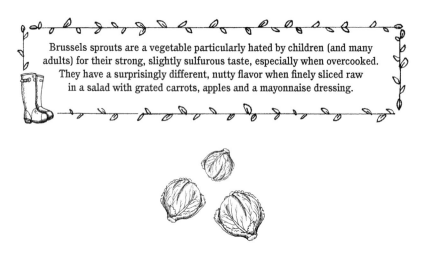

Brussels sprouts are a vegetable particularly hated by children (and many adults) for their strong, slightly sulfurous taste, especially when overcooked. They have a surprisingly different, nutty flavor when finely sliced raw in a salad with grated carrots, apples and a mayonnaise dressing.

PLANT POTATOES ON GOOD FRIDAY

The efficacy of this advice depends on where you live and the timing of Easter. In the south of England a crop is believed to be doomed if planted on that day. In the north, and in the Midlands, where Good Friday is known as "Spud Day," the reverse is true.

Because Easter is a movable feast – it falls on the first Sunday after the first full moon following the vernal equinox (March 21) – planting potatoes on Good Friday will not necessarily guarantee either good weather or warm soil. Advice concerning the moon and potato planting is contradictory, at best, but the majority opinion favors planting when the moon is on the wane (which chimes with Good Friday) but also in darkness before the moon rises or after it sets.

Some country folk still believe that a potato in your pocket will draw out from the body the substances that cause rheumatism.

Before planting, seed potatoes need to be chitted, or sprouted, to start them into growth. Place the "eyes" uppermost in slatted trays in a cool dry place. At planting time, rub off all but the best one or two sprouts with your thumb to concentrate the growth effort of the plant. To help prevent the tubers from developing too near the surface and turning green, earth up the rows after planting, again once the top growth appears, and repeat fortnightly until the flowers open.

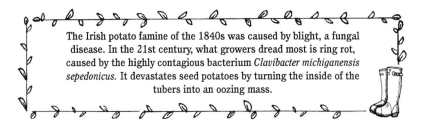

The Irish potato famine of the 1840s was caused by blight, a fungal disease. In the 21st century, what growers dread most is ring rot, caused by the highly contagious bacterium *Clavibacter michiganensis sepedonicus.* It devastates seed potatoes by turning the inside of the tubers into an oozing mass.

DON'T LET RASPBERRIES FRUIT IN THEIR FIRST YEAR

This is wise advice if you're growing summer-fruiting raspberries, which appreciate time to make good root systems before putting their energies into making fruit, but it is not necessary for late cropping varieties planted the previous autumn.

The secret of responding to raspberries' needs lies in the timing. Summer raspberries bear their fruits on shoots produced the previous year. Autumn ones make both shoots and fruits in the same year. Pruning the tops off summer raspberries in their first year encourages the plants to make strong, fruit-bearing shoots in their second.

Plant care also depends on the season. The fruit-bearing stems of early raspberries should be cut back to a few inches from the ground after the harvest is completed. By contrast all the stems of autumn-fruiting varieties need cutting in late autumn or early spring, before the new season's shoots emerge. Leaving the tops on through the winter gives the plants some protection from frost.

The botanical name for the raspberry fruit is an etaerio, which describes a cluster of small, fleshy fruits (druplets), each containing an individual stone or pip.

Because they are shallow-rooted, all raspberries appreciate support, shelter and an absence of weeds, which suck vital water from the soil if left to grow. A bark or leaf mulch spread after the raspberries have been well watered will help to conserve moisture and suppress most weeds.

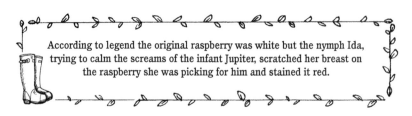

According to legend the original raspberry was white but the nymph Ida, trying to calm the screams of the infant Jupiter, scratched her breast on the raspberry she was picking for him and stained it red.

NEVER GROW LABURNUM IN A GARDEN WHERE CHILDREN PLAY

••

Laburnum seeds, which look very much like peas, are attractive to children but deadly poisonous. If you already have a laburnum in your garden, warn children to stay well away from the pods and seeds.

Its spring covering of long strings of yellow pea-like flowers gives the laburnum its common names of golden chain, golden rain and watch and chain. Within about five years the most popular garden variety, *Laburnum x watereri* 'Vossii' – which has the advantage of producing only a sparse number of seeds – will grow to a height of about 20 feet (6 m).

> *Old-fashioned antidotes for laburnum poisoning were strong coffee and sal volatile (ammonia).*

In the wild, the two species of laburnum *L. alpinum* and *L. anagyroides* ("Vossii" is a result of a cross between them) are found from France eastwards to Hungary. Both the wild species can be found in British hedgerows, where they are thought to have been planted deliberately, possibly to attract honey bees but probably for their wood, which has long been prized for its unique grain pattern. Cut into thin strips it is traditionally incorporated into ornamental inlays and veneers.

Other poisonous plants to grow with caution if you have children are foxgloves, yew, juniper and hellebores, which are all toxic if eaten. And beware of euphorbias, which (except for *E. pulcherrima*) exude a milky white sap that can severely irritate eyes and skin.

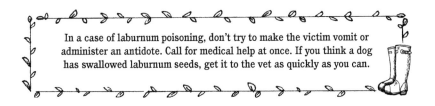

In a case of laburnum poisoning, don't try to make the victim vomit or administer an antidote. Call for medical help at once. If you think a dog has swallowed laburnum seeds, get it to the vet as quickly as you can.

LEEKS ARE GREEDY FEEDERS

These vegetables certainly need plenty of food if they are to grow to a generous size, although the champion leek growers of Britain's northeast keep their secret fertilizer formula well guarded.

Rich, fertile soil, well composted during late autumn, is the starting point for a good leek crop, but these vegetables will also appreciate a dressing of superphosphate given at 1 ounce per square yard (30 g/sq m) and potassium sulfate at half that dosage, lightly forked into the soil in late spring before the pencil-thick young plants, about 8 inches (20 cm), are set out.

The Romans revered the leek as the most prized member of the onion family. The Emperor Nero, who believed that eating them would improve his singing, ate leeks in such quantity that he was nicknamed "Porrophagus," the leek eater.

Leeks (*Allium porrum*) fare well when planted out the traditional way: make dibber holes about 6 inches (15 cm) deep and drop the plants in. Water them well but do not fill the empty part of the hole with soil. Some gardeners trim the tops of the plants to cut down water loss but this is really only necessary in very hot weather.

As the leeks grow, feed them regularly with a liquid feed or top dress with concentrated manure. In autumn, earth up the plants to maximize the length of the white part of each leek.

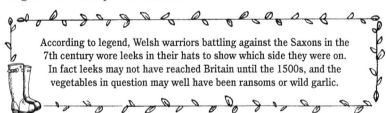

According to legend, Welsh warriors battling against the Saxons in the 7th century wore leeks in their hats to show which side they were on. In fact leeks may not have reached Britain until the 1500s, and the vegetables in question may well have been ransoms or wild garlic.

ONE YEAR'S SEED, SEVEN YEARS' WEED

Not just an exhortation to get weeds out of the ground before they set seed, but also testament to the quantity and longevity of the seeds that weed plants produce. Weed seeds are at their very worst, however, when they germinate into perennial pests that also multiply below ground.

Common annual weeds such as chickweed (*Stellaria media*), fat hen (*Chenopodium album*) and groundsel (*Senecio vulgaris*) are successful because they produce a profusion of seeds that germinate quickly and easily in any soil, maturing to make yet more seeds that, unlike many others, do not need months of dormancy before bursting into life again. They are hardy, too,

Although poppies have grown as weeds in cornfields since Neolithic times, it is an ancient belief that they should not be picked because they protect crops against torrential summer rains.

often flourishing through the winter. Other seeds, like those of the field poppy (*Papaver rhoeas*), produced by the thousand in a single head, will lie dormant for years until the soil is disturbed, as happened during World War I on the battlefields of Flanders.

But annual weeds – especially if hoed from your beds before they set seed – are relatively easy to eradicate compared with perennials. With bindweed (*Convolvulus arvensis*), creeping buttercups (*Ranunculus repens*), horsetails (*Equisetum arvense*) and their like, dogged persistence, if not chemical warfare, is the only way to stop your valuable plants from getting choked.

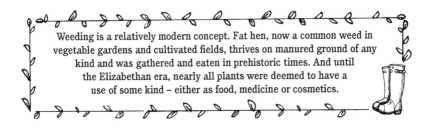

Weeding is a relatively modern concept. Fat hen, now a common weed in vegetable gardens and cultivated fields, thrives on manured ground of any kind and was gathered and eaten in prehistoric times. And until the Elizabethan era, nearly all plants were deemed to have a use of some kind – either as food, medicine or cosmetics.

PLANT GARLIC ON THE SHORTEST DAY AND HARVEST IT ON THE LONGEST

• •

A good way of saying that, like other bulbs, garlic will survive the winter and produce its crop in summer. In fact cloves can be planted from mid autumn to mid winter, before hard frosts set in.

Individual cloves from a single head of garlic (*Allium sativum*) pushed no more than 2 inches (5 cm) into the soil will provide a dozen or more plants. Underground, the single clove multiplies itself into a complete new head. By midsummer's day, or soon after, when the top growth begins to die down, you can start eating the new season's crop. Known as "wet garlic," it has a wonderfully mild flavor. For keeping, pull

Garlic is a powerful antiseptic; the French used it to clean soldiers' wounds during World War I.

up the heads, dry them off for about two weeks, then tie or plait the leaves together to make strings and hang them up in a cool dry place. If you find pure garlic too strong for salads, try growing milder-tasting white-flowered garlic chives (*A. tuberosum*) in the herb garden or herbaceous border.

Garlic's name comes from "gar," meaning spear (which refers to the shape of the leaves) and "leak," the old spelling of leek. Although it likes to be kept well watered in spring during dry spells, wet weather can make it vulnerable to white rot, a fungal disease that destroys the bulbs. It is almost impossible to treat and experts say that following such an infection plants of the onion family should not be grown on the same soil for eight years.

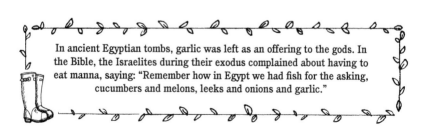

In ancient Egyptian tombs, garlic was left as an offering to the gods. In the Bible, the Israelites during their exodus complained about having to eat manna, saying: "Remember how in Egypt we had fish for the asking, cucumbers and melons, leeks and onions and garlic."

IN OCTOBER, MANURE YOUR FIELD AND YOUR LAND ITS WEALTH SHALL YIELD

· ·

Or your garden, especially the vegetable plot. Manuring in autumn gives the compost time to break down over the winter, before seeds are planted in the spring. But a very wet winter may leech much of the goodness from the manure, so you may need to add fertilizer or a proprietary concentrated manure before planting.

You can buy compost or make your own, depending on convenience and the size of your plot. Well-rotted farmyard or stable manure is always good if you can get it, particularly if you need to improve the quality of light or clay soil, as it adds bulk as well as nutrients. For a smaller plot, bags of concentrated manure are a good alternative, although they lack bulk.

In the days of the horse and cart children were routinely sent out into the street with shovels and buckets to gather fresh, steaming "muck" for the garden – especially the rhubarb patch.

It is easy enough to make your own compost, but it is wise to rot fallen leaves separately as they can take several years to break down. Keep your compost heap well watered, especially in dry weather, aerate it regularly by turning the material to speed decomposition. Adding a commercial compost accelerator is also helpful.

Add compost to the soil when you double dig – put it in the lower part of the trench – or add it as a top dressing. You will be surprised by how quickly earthworms will pull the compost downwards, and mix it into the soil.

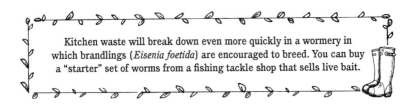

Kitchen waste will break down even more quickly in a wormery in which brandlings (*Eisenia foetida*) are encouraged to breed. You can buy a "starter" set of worms from a fishing tackle shop that sells live bait.

ADD THESE TO A COMPOST HEAP	AVOID
 Annual weeds	Perennial weeds
Lawn mowings	Fallen leaves
Vegetable peelings, eggshells	Meat and bones (can attract vermin)
Shredded newspaper	Glossy magazine pages, cardboard
Coffee grounds and tea leaves	Banana peel (slow to rot)
Healthy withered leaves, prunings, rhubarb leaves	Diseased stems, roots, leaves and fruit

WHITEWASH YOUR GREENHOUSE IN SUMMER

Or, even better, once the weather starts warming up in late spring, to protect plants from the scorching effects of the sun. Before painted-on shading became popular, greenhouses were fitted on the outsides of their roofs with adjustable wooden blinds.

What you need for this job is proprietary water-soluble white shading or limewash, not the sort of whitewash you would use indoors for your walls. Ideally it needs to be brushed on in late spring and sponged off again in autumn. As well as shading, the plants in the summer greenhouse need to be well watered and given plenty of ventilation. These two tasks can now easily be automated. Ventilator mechanisms work by means of expanding latches that open the greenhouse windows when heated.

The Romans used sheets of the mineral mica to protect and warm their plants, particularly melons, cucumbers and other tender edibles.

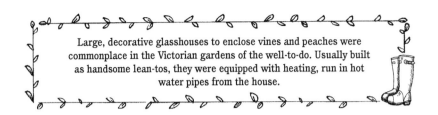

Large, decorative glasshouses to enclose vines and peaches were commonplace in the Victorian gardens of the well-to-do. Usually built as handsome lean-tos, they were equipped with heating, run in hot water pipes from the house.

In hot weather greenhouse plants appreciate extra humidity. You can supply this by spraying the greenhouse benches with water. Another idea is to hang up a towel with its end in a bowl of water, which will be absorbed then evaporate.

One of the most famous glasshouses ever built was the lily house at Chatsworth in Derbyshire, made for the Duke of Devonshire in the 1840s by Joseph Paxton. Its design was based on the natural ribbing in the leaf of the giant Victoria waterlily. Paxton went on to use the same principles in the construction of the world renowned Crystal Palace for the Great Exhibition that was held in London in 1851.

WATER PLANTS WELL OR NOT AT ALL

This is good advice, because just a little water will dampen only the top layer of soil and can encourage plants to develop roots near the surface. Too many of these shallow roots will make the plants liable to wind damage and unable to absorb sufficient nutrients from the soil.

The roots of a plant will extend healthily downwards (influenced by gravity) and outwards in their search for water, and a good soaking once a week will usually suffice, especially if your soil has been improved with water-retaining compost (see "In October, Manure Your Field and Your Land Its Wealth Shall Yield" on page 87). As you water, be sure to direct moisture to the roots of plants, not on to their leaves. This is not just economical but helps to prevent water drops from acting as miniature lenses, which in summer can concentrate the sun's rays and mar foliage with unsightly scorch marks.

Water seedlings and small plants carefully. All but the finest water spray can damage or even uproot them. For thirsty plants such as cucumbers and tomatoes, sink a terracotta flowerpot or an inverted plastic bottle with its bottom cut off next to each one. You can then pour water into the receptacle and be sure that it is all going directly to the roots rather than evaporating from the soil surface.

Prevent container plants from becoming waterlogged by putting in plenty of drainage material such as broken pieces of terracotta or polystyrene chips before you add soil.

Time of day is important. Evening watering is best in summer, to minimize evaporation. When the weather is cooler it is best to water in the morning, as this prevents it from freezing overnight and damaging plants.

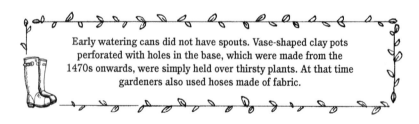

Early watering cans did not have spouts. Vase-shaped clay pots perforated with holes in the base, which were made from the 1470s onwards, were simply held over thirsty plants. At that time gardeners also used hoses made of fabric.

PLANT VEGETABLES WITH EDIBLE LEAVES WHEN THE MOON IS WANING

According to one piece of ancient lore this moon-based timing will stop the plants becoming full of sap and consequently running quickly to seed. By contrast, it is said, plants with edible roots, which need to be juicy, should be planted when the moon is waxing. Only trial and error can prove or disprove either saying.

Most popular lunar gardening advice, however, totally contradicts these maxims, recommending that plants that produce their edible parts above ground should be sown or planted during the increasing light of the moon (from new to full) and those that produce food below ground should be sown or planted when the moon's light is decreasing night by night.

Probably since the establishment of the earliest human societies, the moon has influenced our behavior. One of the earliest references linking gardening with the moon's phases was made by Pliny the Elder, who wrote in his *Natural History XVIII* in AD 77: "All vegetable productions are cut, gathered, and housed to more advantage while the moon is on the wane," and "It is generally recommended…to make seed-plots when the moon is above the horizon."

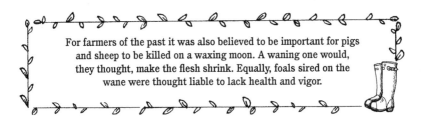

For farmers of the past it was also believed to be important for pigs and sheep to be killed on a waxing moon. A waning one would, they thought, make the flesh shrink. Equally, foals sired on the wane were thought liable to lack health and vigor.

OTHER LUNAR GARDENING TIPS

- Plant nothing on the day of a new or full moon.
- Gather mushrooms when the moon is young and rising.
- Weed by moonlight – the shadow of your hoe will stop the weeds growing again.
- Prune fruit trees in spring when the moon is waxing and they will not be damaged by frost.
- To encourage your lawn to grow fast, cut it during the first quarter of the moon.

PLANT PEARS FOR YOUR HEIRS

Pears can take up to 20 years to fruit when planted from seed, but trees can also last well over a century. Since few pears are self-fertile you will need two plants (they can be different varieties) that flower at the same time to ensure a good crop.

The best pears for most modern gardens are those grafted on quince rootstocks, which keep the size of the trees under control and produce fruit more quickly. Compared with apples, pears appreciate more sun and general warmth, and a more fertile, loamy soil. A sheltered spot will also help to protect the early spring blossom from wind and ensure pollination.

Over the centuries more than a thousand varieties of pear have been bred. For cooking, the Warden

The pear (Pyrus spp) originated, like the apple, in the Caucasus and was long considered the superior fruit, especially by the Greeks and Romans. "Natural" ungrafted trees can grow to 21 feet (7 m) or more.

pear, bred by Cistercian monks in Berkshire in medieval times and also known as the Shakespeare, was a kitchen staple until the plethora of plant breeding that took place in the 16th and 17th centuries resulted in sweeter, less gritty, eaters.

Pears were first grown in the USA after the Massachusetts Company imported seeds from England in 1629. The William pear, first grown in Berkshire in 1770 by John Stair, a schoolmaster, is known in America as the Bartlett after Enoch Bartlett, who took it there in the following century. The Seckel, a spicy American pear, is said to have been discovered by a trapper in 1765 on a piece of land he had purchased.

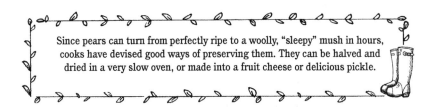

Since pears can turn from perfectly ripe to a woolly, "sleepy" mush in hours, cooks have devised good ways of preserving them. They can be halved and dried in a very slow oven, or made into a fruit cheese or delicious pickle.

KITCHEN TIPS

As if by instinct, good cooks seem to know how to make everything turn out right. Their bread and cakes always rise, their sauces never curdle. But as well as hours and hours of practice, the best cooks rely on the advice handed down by previous generations.

The oldest known recipes were inscribed on stone tablets in Mesopotamia in about 1700 BC. The only cookbook known from the classical world is that of Apicius from the 1st century AD, but the publishing of practical advice for home cooks really began in 1747 with *The Art of Cookery Made Plain and Easy* by the English author Hannah Glasse. The baton was taken up in Britain by Eliza Acton in her *Modern Cookery for Private Families* of 1845 and Isabella Beeton, whose *Beeton's Book of Household Management* of 1861 remains a classic. But the American cook Fannie Merritt Farmer was determined to leave nothing to chance. As principal, she created *The Boston Cooking-School Cookbook* in 1896, with recipes measured accurately to the level teaspoon, tablespoon and cup.

Technology has transformed the kitchen since the days of the kitchen range but however food is prepared, it is never more true than in cookery that attention to detail and practice make perfect.

TO SAVE SEPARATED MAYONNAISE, ADD ANOTHER EGG

The 19th-century American perfectionist Fannie Merritt Farmer offered this sound advice, as have many good cooks before and since, although hot water is also recommended by some.

Mayonnaise, a fine emulsion of egg yolks and oil, is made by adding oil drop by drop to yolks mixed with some salt, while beating vigorously and continuously. What happens as you mix is that the oil is broken into smaller and smaller droplets, which eventually stabilize into a rich, thick mixture. Adding the oil too fast, or insufficient beating, are usually what makes the mixture separate out, so that pools of oil form, making the mixture look curdled. Keeping cool is, in every sense, critical to the process (and the sanity of the cook), because it makes everything more stable.

"Smooth consistency," says Miss Farmer, "may be restored by taking the yolk of another egg and adding curdled mixture to it." And she adds, "It is desirable to have bowl containing mixture placed in a larger bowl of crushed ice, to which a small quantity of water has been added."

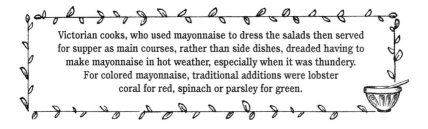

Victorian cooks, who used mayonnaise to dress the salads then served for supper as main courses, rather than side dishes, dreaded having to make mayonnaise in hot weather, especially when it was thundery. For colored mayonnaise, traditional additions were lobster coral for red, spinach or parsley for green.

WIPE, DON'T WASH, MUSHROOMS

The theory behind this age-old advice is that washing mushrooms makes them soggy, but since they are already 90 percent water, a little more is not likely to make much difference.

Irish folklore maintains that if you see a button mushroom you should pluck it, as it will not grow any more once it has been looked at.

The preparation method, therefore, is the cook's prerogative, although the tenacity with which pieces of dirt cling to the cups often makes washing the only practical cleaning method. Careful brushing is also effective. Peeling today's cultivated mushrooms is almost always unnecessary, but may improve large field mushrooms that have been gathered from the wild. For fine dishes the stalks of mushrooms are best removed, and the frugal cook will keep them for flavoring stocks or stews.

Most of the mushrooms we cook and eat today are cultivated – and have been since the 17th century, when the French discovered how to "sow" the underground filaments or mycelia from which the mushrooms grew in beds of asses' dung.

Mushrooms were traditionally stewed with butter and served under roast poultry or, in the 19th century, presented stuffed as an entrée. As a savory – a dish eaten at the end of an English dinner during the 19th and early 20th centuries – mushrooms on toast was a popular choice.

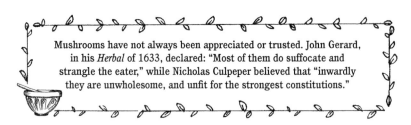

Mushrooms have not always been appreciated or trusted. John Gerard, in his *Herbal* of 1633, declared: "Most of them do suffocate and strangle the eater," while Nicholas Culpeper believed that "inwardly they are unwholesome, and unfit for the strongest constitutions."

STEW BOILED IS A STEW SPOILED

Long and low is the cook's guide for guaranteeing tender meat in stews and casseroles. If the pot is allowed to boil hard the meat will become stringy because the muscle fibers of which meat is composed shrink quickly, making them tough.

The stew has long been favored by both busy and cost-conscious cooks. It can be left to simmer untended on a low heat, and can make even the most economical cuts palatable. As the meat cooks, the tough collagen – the tissue that holds the bundles of muscle fibers together – is broken down into succulent gelatin. At the same time, the fat in the meat melts, deliciously infusing any pulses, potatoes or root vegetables added to the pot with its flavor.

For a fish stew, such as the flavoursome Mediterranean bouillabaisse, gentle heat is needed not for tenderizing the ingredients but to make sure that the fish does not disintegrate into the cooking liquid.

Stews have their origins in the tradition of cooking over an open fire, the particular ingredients depending on local agriculture and climate. In an Irish stew, neck of mutton or kid are the key ingredients, plus potatoes, onions and a little water. No carrots, barley, leeks or other ingredients should, purists argue, be added, and when the stew is cooked all the liquid should have been absorbed by the potatoes, converting them into a thick, creamy mash.

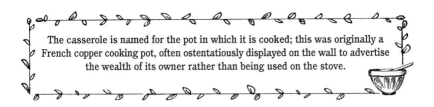

The casserole is named for the pot in which it is cooked; this was originally a French copper cooking pot, often ostentatiously displayed on the wall to advertise the wealth of its owner rather than being used on the stove.

HEAT A LEMON BEFORE YOU SQUEEZE IT

An old cook's tip made even easier if you have a microwave and just as effective for limes, too. Just 30 seconds on "high" will soften the fruit's internal membranes. Five minutes in a warm oven works equally well.

L emon juice is one of the cook's essential ingredients, for everything from a marinade to tenderize meat to a flavoring for a cake, so it makes sense to get every last drop of juice from the fruit. As well as applying gentle heat, another good way to help release maximum juice from a lemon or lime is to roll it backwards and forwards on a work surface a few times before squeezing it.

Be positive: when life deals you lemons, make lemonade.

Old-fashioned mechanical lemon squeezers come in two basic designs: the hand-held wooden "reamer" and the glass pyramid molded in a dish to catch the juice with protrusions to trap any pips and pulp. One ingenious 1930s device for extracting just a few drops of juice consisted of a perforated aluminium tube that was pushed into the lemon before the fruit was gently squeezed.

Lemons were an expensive rarity until the 16th century, when the Italians began growing them in quantity and the Spanish planted the first lemon groves in California. Even when this rich lemon cheesecake recipe was written in the 1740s, in the *Compleat Housewife of Williamsburg, Virginia*, lemons would still have been a luxury: "Take two large lemons, grate off the peel of both and squeeze out the juice of one; add it to half a pound of fine sugar; twelve yolks of eggs, eight egg whites well beaten; then melt half a pound of butter in four or five spoonfuls of cream; then stir it all together, and set it over the fire, stirring 'til it be pretty thick…when 'tis cold, fill your patty-pans little more than half full; put a fine paste very thin at the bottom…half an hour, with a quick oven, will bake them."

ALWAYS PEEL ONIONS UNDER WATER

Immersion is good for two reasons. For large onions, cold water can stop them making you cry. For small pickling onions or shallots, boiling water loosens stubborn skins and eases peeling.

Peeling onions makes your eyes stream because they give off the volatile substances pyruvic acid and allicin (called lachrymators) when their tissues are cut. When these meet the fluid in the eye they create a weak – but stinging – solution. Under cold running water, the lachrymators have the chance of dissolving before they can get to the eyes.

Keeping cut onions in the house has long been said to be unlucky because it was believed that the cut surface would absorb impurities from the air and "breed distempers."

For slicing and chopping, however, there is no alternative to bearing the pain, but it may help to cool onions in the refrigerator before you cut them; this makes the lachrymators a little less volatile. Also if you have contact lenses, wear them while preparing onions and you'll cry a lot less. Or look out for "Supasweet" onions, bred to have a much lower pyruvic acid content than regular types.

The fiery chemical components of onions are quickly and easily subdued by cooking. When heated, the volatile odors are dissipated; some are converted, for our pleasure, into sugar, others into chemicals more than 50 times sweeter. It is this sweetness that makes the tear-jerking preparation of a French onion stew worthwhile, and onions so indispensable.

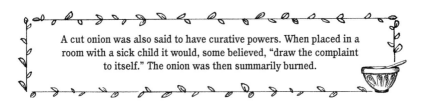

A cut onion was also said to have curative powers. When placed in a room with a sick child it would, some believed, "draw the complaint to itself." The onion was then summarily burned.

SALT SEASONS ALL THINGS

Not only savory foods but sweet ones, such as cakes and pastries, need salt. The cook's essential for flavor has also been used for millennia as a food preservative.

No kitchen is complete without salt, simple sodium chloride, the white, crystalline chemical that comes from seawater, which is also mined worldwide. As well as improving the taste of every savory dish, a pinch of salt added to the flour in a cake or sweet pastry mixture improves the balance of flavors. When added to acid fruits such as pineapple and grapefruit, it even enhances their sweetness.

The world's best known salted foods include salt cod, the fiel amigo *(faithful friend) of the Portuguese, sauerkraut, bacon and salami.*

Adjust the seasoning before you serve a dish but remember that many people are now deliberately lowering their sodium intake for health reasons. If in doubt, undersalt the dish and let guests add extra at the table. Don't forget that saltiness changes with temperature. A perfectly salted hot leek and potato soup will seem tasteless and bland when chilled as a vichyssoise.

Sea salt is the kind most prized by connoisseurs, especially when made by evaporating seawater in the sun. Ordinary table salt is treated with small amounts of magnesium carbonate to keep it flowing freely. It may also be iodized – that is, have the mineral iodine added as a health benefit.

Preserving food with salt goes back to the Egyptian practice of salting fish in the 3rd millennium BC and became the norm in Iron Age Britain. It works by drawing out water, in which microbes flourish, and by killing any that do survive. By the Middle Ages, salt fish was Britain's standard fare. After salting, fish were also dried and smoked to become "red herrings," which would keep undecayed for a whole year.

A SOUFFLÉ COOKED TOO FAST WILL BE FULL OF HOLES

The art of the hot soufflé comes down to confident mixing, careful cooking and immediate serving. When it succeeds, few dishes are more spectacular or delicious.

The scientific secret behind the soufflé lies in the creation of a foam of stiffly beaten egg whites that is folded into sauce made from butter, flour and the egg yolks. When this mixture is heated two things happen. The air trapped in the egg white foam expands and the proteins in the egg change from liquid to solid – they set. In the perfect soufflé the setting point and the moment of maximum foam expansion coincide.

The cheese soufflé is the classic savory version; hot chocolate, lemon and fruit are the sweet equivalents. However, a cold soufflé, set with gelatin, is more like a mousse.

If the oven is too hot the egg will set too quickly, creating a solid soufflé full of holes. If it is too cold the center will not set properly and be too liquid. The ideal oven setting is 350°F/180°C/ Gas mark 4. To prevent it cooking too quickly, place the dish in a pan of hot water to come about halfway up the side before putting it in the oven.

Resist, above all, the temptation to open the oven door while the soufflé is cooking. A rush of cold air will prevent the air in the mixture from expanding properly. Equally, a soufflé left standing once out of the oven will quickly begin to collapse as the air inside cools and contracts.

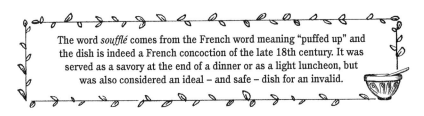

The word *soufflé* comes from the French word meaning "puffed up" and the dish is indeed a French concoction of the late 18th century. It was served as a savory at the end of a dinner or as a light luncheon, but was also considered an ideal – and safe – dish for an invalid.

ALWAYS ADD SALT TO PORRIDGE

Of all the foods whose flavor is enhanced by salt, porridge comes to the top. But how much salt to add is a matter of taste. Purists insist on their morning booster being a savory dish, not one sweetened with sugar, honey or even fresh fruit.

Although porridge is a general word for any "mush" made with cereals such as oats or oatmeal, barley, rye, hominy or even polenta, it is the Scots who claim the dish – made with oats – as their own, and regard salt as a key ingredient. No self-respecting Scot, it is said, will allow any other addition but milk or cream. Sugar is strictly for children.

Before the introduction of "instant oats," porridge making was a ritual that demanded the use of a special stirrer known as a spurtle or "porridge stick." Water was put on to boil, oatmeal sprinkled in with the left hand and the porridge stirred with the right. In this, it is said, "consists the art of porridge making, as on it being well done depends the absence of lumps

By tradition, Highland Scots would set porridge in a mould – which was often a sideboard drawer – and cut it into chunks, when cold, to take out with them for sustenance throughout the day.

or knots... Boil 10 minutes, then add salt and boil 10 minutes longer. It is best not to put the salt in till the end of 10 minutes as it has a tendency to harden the meal and prevent its fully expanding."

Porridge is sustaining because oats have a low glycemic index. This means that they are digested slowly, keeping blood sugar levels steady over a long period and making them an ideal food for diabetics and athletes taking part in endurance exercise. And because they contain soluble fiber, oats can help lower your cholesterol level.

STOP AVOCADOS GOING BROWN WITH LEMON JUICE

....

Not just avocados. The lemon juice trick – or lime juice if you prefer – works just as effectively on apples, pears and bananas. The secret lies in the acid that these citrus fruits contain.

Cutting an avocado sets to work the enzyme polyphenol oxidase, which in the presence of oxygen in the air creates brown compounds in the flesh. The citric acid in lemon juice slows the action of the enzyme to a snail's pace. The acetic acid in an oil and vinegar dressing has a similar effect, as does ascorbic acid or vitamin C, first isolated in 1925 by a Hungarian biochemist Albert Szent-Györgyi, who perceptively noticed that the juice of a fruit that does not brown in air can delay the discoloration of one that does.

The avocado or avocado pear (*Persea americana*) is unique among fruits for its high fat content of up to 30 percent, which has earned it the nickname "poor man's butter." And

An avocado will never ripen until after it has been picked or becomes a windfall. A biochemical inhibitor in the tree is thought to prevent the ripening process.

although avocados contain up to 400 calories per fruit, the fat is the "good" monounsaturated sort that is thought to help lower blood cholesterol levels.

In subtropical America, archaeologists have traced avocado cultivation back more than 7,000 years. All today's fruits are descended from three original races: the purple, smooth-skinned Mexican; the rough-skinned Guatemalan; and the large, smooth West Indian.

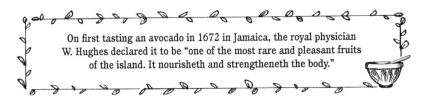

On first tasting an avocado in 1672 in Jamaica, the royal physician W. Hughes declared it to be "one of the most rare and pleasant fruits of the island. It nourisheth and strengtheneth the body."

FOR PASTRY: COOL WHILE MAKING, HOT WHILE BAKING

•••

This is undoubtedly the key to success with everyday shortcrust or "plain" pastry, and for flaky and puff pastry. The exceptions are fancy pastries such as choux and the hot water crust used for authentic pork and game pies.

In making shortcrust pastry, coolness is vital to prevent sticky gluten in the flour from developing and to keep the particles of fat (lard, butter or a mixture of the two) from becoming liquid and thus a less effective barrier between the grains of flour. To keep everything as cool as possible, use chilled fat, cut it into the flour with a knife, then rub it in with the fingertips. Quickly stir in chilled water with a knife, and finish the mixture using the fingers of one hand until it just leaves the sides of the bowl. Half an hour's rest in the refrigerator, followed by rolling of the dough with a marble or glass rolling pin on a cool worktop, are the other essentials for avoiding heat.

Large Victorian kitchens had separate pastry rooms with cool marble tops, which were a boon to cooks in the summer months.

In a hot oven (200°C/400°F/Gas mark 6) the particles of fat or shortening melt but, because they have kept the flour grains separate, long strands of gluten are prevented from forming. Quick, high-temperature cooking also keeps the starch grains in the flour stiff, making the pastry crisp. This, combined with the expansion of air trapped in the mixture and the release of steam as the water in the mixture evaporates, gives the pastry its lightness.

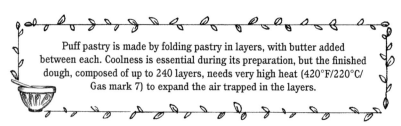

Puff pastry is made by folding pastry in layers, with butter added between each. Coolness is essential during its preparation, but the finished dough, composed of up to 240 layers, needs very high heat (420°F/220°C/ Gas mark 7) to expand the air trapped in the layers.

WHEN MAKING TEA, ADD ONE FOR THE POT

••

Grandmother's dictum results in a good strong brew, but today tea is a matter of taste. However you make it, "a nice cup of tea" has undoubted health benefits, being rich in antioxidants, substances that can help reduce the risk of heart disease.

While tea bags are hard to beat for convenience, the pure taste of a high quality tea can be appreciated only by using leaf tea in a pot. When you pour boiling water on to a black tea (very hot, not boiling, is best for green tea), it releases a variety of substances, including caffeine, essential oils, polyphenols and the tannins that give tea its astringent effect.

According to Chinese legend, in the year 2737 BC the Emperor Shen Nung was resting under a tea tree when the wind blew some leaves into some water he was heating. The resulting drink so refreshed and revitalized him that tea drinking was "invented."

While some people insist that tea's flavor is best (and good manners best satisfied) when tea is put in the cup first, others maintain that it is only possibly to get the strength exactly right if it is added after the milk. The British, who began drinking tea in the 1650s (the merchant Thomas Garraway first sold it at his London store in 1658) were probably the first to add milk, to help soften tea's bitter tannins. Putting the milk in first may have helped to prevent fine Chinese porcelain tea bowls from cracking.

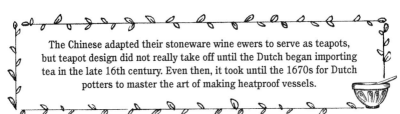

The Chinese adapted their stoneware wine ewers to serve as teapots, but teapot design did not really take off until the Dutch began importing tea in the late 16th century. Even then, it took until the 1670s for Dutch potters to master the art of making heatproof vessels.

STOP MILK BOILING OVER: GREASE THE TOP OF THE PAN WITH BUTTER

Or, even easier, add a large, clean marble, but the failsafe solution is to use a heavy pan on a low to moderate heat and to stir and keep watch over the milk as it warms up. The other advantage of a heavy pan is that it prevents heated milk sticking and burning.

Hot milk can boil over in a second, but if caught at the instant when the froth is just rising it makes the perfect addition to hot chocolate. The grease trick works because it helps to prevent the foam from rising up the pan, but only temporarily. The marble acts as an in-built stirrer, but it, too, is fallible. Frothing milk with a jet of steam – which is what the steamer nozzle on an espresso coffee machine achieves – is an ideal solution, and prevents unpalatable skin forming. When using a pan, stirring the milk helps, although stirring in a skin once it has formed merely spreads the unappetizing bits through the rest of the milk.

A nonstick pan won't stop milk boiling over but will make cleaning easier. Teflon, originally produced in the USA by the DuPont company in 1938, was first used to coat pans in 1955 by the Frenchman Marc Grégoire.

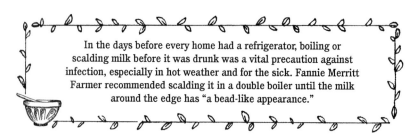

In the days before every home had a refrigerator, boiling or scalding milk before it was drunk was a vital precaution against infection, especially in hot weather and for the sick. Fannie Merritt Farmer recommended scalding it in a double boiler until the milk around the edge has "a bead-like appearance."

ALWAYS ADD VINEGAR TO THE WATER WHEN YOU POACH AN EGG

For the inexperienced cook, this is a sensible precaution to help the egg white seal quickly. Too much vinegar can mar the flavor if the eggs are to be eaten plain, but will be disguised by a sauce.

Making perfectly poached eggs is a culinary art worth mastering. Start with a deep frying pan filled with 3 inches (7.5 cm) of water with, if you wish, 1–2 tablespoons of mild vinegar added. When the water has reached a rolling boil, crack an egg into a part of the water that is bubbling hard so that it spins around in the vortex. (If you are nervous, break the egg into a saucer first, then slide it into the water.) Add more eggs in the same way, then lower the heat to get the gentlest of simmers. In about four minutes the whites should be set and the yolks still runny. Lift out the cooked eggs with a slotted spoon and drain them. Trim away any untidy white around the edges before serving.

Eggs Benedict – an English muffin topped with grilled Canadian bacon (not cold ham), poached eggs, hollandaise sauce and (for sheer luxury) a slice of truffle, has been an American favorite for decades. There are various versions of its origin. One is that Mrs. LeGrand Benedict devised it, in conjunction with the chef at New York's Delmonico's Restaurant, in the 1860s. Another is that in 1894 it was ordered by Lemuel Benedict, a Wall Street broker, when suffering from a hangover.

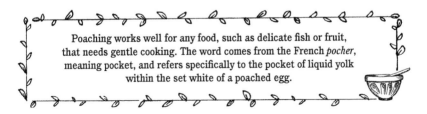

Poaching works well for any food, such as delicate fish or fruit, that needs gentle cooking. The word comes from the French *pocher*, meaning pocket, and refers specifically to the pocket of liquid yolk within the set white of a poached egg.

EAT OYSTERS ONLY WHEN THERE'S AN "R" IN THE MONTH

A catchy way of warning against the possibility of food poisoning from oysters, mussels and other crustaceans in the warmest months (in the northern hemisphere) of May to August, none of which includes a letter "r." Oysters are now bred and farmed to reduce the risk of infection all year.

Oysters feed on microscopic algae that can become infected with bacteria, and these multiply rapidly in warm seawater. Of these, *Vibrio parahaemolyticus* is the most common, causing stomach pains and sickness, but most deadly is *V. vulnificus*, which can bring on septicemia. What's more, eating one bad oyster can sensitize you indefinitely to them all.

Oysters were so abundant in England in the early 19th century that they were regarded as poor people's food. Sam Weller, in Charles Dickens's The Pickwick Papers, *declares that "poverty and oysters always seem to go together."*

A "good" oyster should always be tightly closed when you buy it and should open when it is cooked. If it is to be eaten raw, an oyster must be scrubbed clean then prized open with an oyster knife. Cooks would traditionally keep live oysters in the kitchen for a few days and feed them with oatmeal to fatten them and make them more luscious. The smallest of them were saved for eating raw, larger ones cooked and added to steak pies or turkey stuffing, made into patties or dipped in batter and fried.

The reputation of oysters as an aphrodisiac (the famed 18th-century Italian lover Casanova is said to have eaten 40 a day) may be justified by their mineral content as well as their looks and texture. They are rich in zinc, a substance essential to sperm production.

YOU CAN'T MAKE BREAD IN A COLD KITCHEN

Unless, that is, you are making unleavened bread or soda bread, which needs no yeast. Warmth is essential to the "magic" of bread making; it allows the live yeast cells to multiply and, as they do so, produce the carbon dioxide gas that makes the mixture rise.

Yeast (*Saccharoymyces cerevisiae*) is a single-celled fungus that is fussy about warmth. Below 70°F (21°C) its cells reproduce only very slowly. Above about 130°F (56°C) they die. The temperature at which they grow fastest and most steadily is just above human body temperature, at 100°F (38°C). *Candida* yeast, which produces the lactic acid that gives sourdough bread its characteristic flavor, needs a similar temperature.

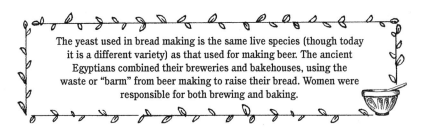

The yeast used in bread making is the same live species (though today it is a different variety) as that used for making beer. The ancient Egyptians combined their breweries and bakehouses, using the waste or "barm" from beer making to raise their bread. Women were responsible for both brewing and baking.

Cooling bread is as important to perfection as cooking, because it ensures that water migrates to the crust and does not make the crumb doughy and leathery. Mrs. Beeton advises strongly

The seemingly miraculous properties of yeast led to its medieval name of "goddisgoode" – because it was said to have come from "the great grace of God."

against eating newly cooked bread. "It should," she says, "be carefully shunned by everybody who has the slightest respect for that much-injured individual – the Stomach."

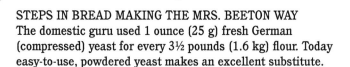

STEPS IN BREAD MAKING THE MRS. BEETON WAY
The domestic guru used 1 ounce (25 g) fresh German (compressed) yeast for every 3½ pounds (1.6 kg) flour. Today easy-to-use, powdered yeast makes an excellent substitute.

1. Mix yeast with ¼ pint (450 ml) of warm milk-and-water and mix until "smooth as cream."
2. Put the flour in a bowl with a pinch of salt and make a well in the middle. Pour in the yeast mixture and stir to make a "thick batter in which there must be no lumps."
3. Sprinkle plenty of flour on top and cover with a thick, clean cloth. "Set it where the air is warm" but not "upon the kitchen fender, for it will be too much heated there" until bubbles break through the flour.
4. Pour in a further ½ pint (300 ml) warm milk-and-water. Throw on plenty of flour, then knead well "with the knuckles of both hands" until the mixture is smooth. It is ready when it "does not stick to the hands when touched."
5. Leave to rise again, for ¾ hour. When it has risen and is beginning to crack, quickly cut into shapes and bake at once in a hot oven.

DON'T OPEN THE OVEN DOOR WHILE A CAKE IS COOKING

••

Especially important for sponge cakes, which like soufflés won't rise properly if subjected to a blast of cold air. For a perfect result the oven needs to be heated to the correct temperature before the cake is put inside.

A "true" sponge cake rises because the air whisked into it expands in the heat of the oven. Classic whisked fatless sponges are the Savoy, in which egg yolks are first beaten with sugar, and the egg whites then beaten until stiff and folded in separately, and the Génoise, in which whole eggs are used. For both, flour is folded in at the end of mixing.

In a creamed sponge, such as a Victoria sponge or sandwich, butter and caster sugar are creamed together until soft and fluffy, then eggs, flour and baking powder added. When heated, the flour produces pockets of carbon dioxide in the mixture. Both this gas and the expanded, heated air beaten into the cake will contract quickly if the oven door is opened and cold air rushes in.

Until the gas cooker made its entry into kitchens from the 1890s cooks were at the mercy of the range, which although it had ventilators to help control the fierceness and heat of the fire was hit and miss for cake making. The manufacturers of gas cookers were quick to produce recipe books to accompany their stoves; the 1930s *Parkinson Cookery Book* boasts that "cakes carefully prepared and put into a controlled oven heated to the correct temperature and given the right time cannot be failures."

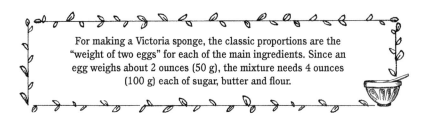

For making a Victoria sponge, the classic proportions are the "weight of two eggs" for each of the main ingredients. Since an egg weighs about 2 ounces (50 g), the mixture needs 4 ounces (100 g) each of sugar, butter and flour.

TO STOP PASTA STICKING, ADD A SPOONFUL OF OIL TO THE COOKING WATER

This can be a wise precaution for fresh pasta, which tends to be stickier than the dried variety, but it is a method that is heartily despised by both Italians and professional cooks.

No pasta is likely to stick if it is cooked in plenty of salted water. For cooking allow, as a rule of thumb, 7 pints (3 liters) of water and a tablespoon of salt for 1 pound (450 g) of dried pasta, with an extra 1¾ pints (1 liter) for every additional 8 ounces (225 g). Plunging the pasta into this generous amount of boiling water allows it to come quickly back to the boil, helps the pieces to stay separate and gives it enough room to swell up.

It is said that spaghetti is ready to eat when it will stick in place if thrown at the wall, but more conventionally it should be timed to be *al dente* or with bite. (The expression literally means "to the tooth.") This may take up to 12 minutes for dried pasta but only three, or less, for fresh.

Marco Polo, who arrived in Venice from his travels to the East in 1298, did not introduce pasta to Italy. The evidence: a "basketful of macaroni" listed in the estate of one Ponzio Bastone in 1279. That this was obviously dried, not fresh pasta, proves, say food historians, that pasta making already had a long tradition in Italy. In fact pasta was probably "invented" independently by both the ancient Chinese and the Etruscans in about the 4th century BC.

Macaroni was almost certainly the first pasta enjoyed in the West. Macaroni cheese, still the ultimate comfort food, featured in British recipe books from the Middle Ages onwards. And although Spanish settlers had brought pasta to America, Thomas Jefferson was so delighted by the macaroni that he ate in Paris in the 1780s that he brought two crates back home with him.

The song by Edward Bangs, first printed in England in 1778 and in America in 1794 (though possibly sung by British troops in the Anglo-French conflict of 1755–63) is testament to the popularity of pasta.

Yankee Doodle came to town
Riding on a pony
Stuck a feather in his cap
And called it Macaroni.

PASTA VARIETIES
Of the dozens of different pasta shapes, some have wonderfully descriptive names that relate to their shapes:

Capelli d'angelo – *angel hair or little hairs* – is the thinnest kind of spaghetti.
Capelletti – *small hats* – stuffed pasta twisted into shapes like three-cornered hats.
Farfalle – resembling butterflies.
Lingune di passero – *sparrows' tongues* – a kind of thin, oval spaghetti.
Maltagliati – *badly cut* – long narrow diamond or triangular shapes.
Orecchiette – *little ears* – shaped as their name describes.
Vermicelli – *small worms* – thin spaghetti, not as thin as angel hair.

TEST AN EGG FOR FRESHNESS BY PUTTING IT IN WATER

In cold water, a fresh egg will sink and lie level on the bottom of the bowl; a stale one – in which gas has accumulated – will float. This sure-fire test was first recorded by the English cook Hannah Glasse, the first "celebrity chef," in 1750.

A less reliable test is to hold the egg up to a bright light. The shell is almost transparent and it will be possible to distinguish the yolk and the white. A stale egg is more translucent at the ends than in the middle, while in a fresh egg the reverse is true.

Even a fresh egg can harbor **Salmonella** *bacteria. To avoid the risk of infection, which can be dangerous to the young, the pregnant, the elderly and infirm, never eat eggs raw, and always cook them until the yolk is set.*

The key to these simple tests is that an egg begins to change as soon as it leaves the hen's body because it continues to "breathe," releasing carbon dioxide gas. Gradually, the white and yolk change, too. The white becomes thinner and the membrane or sac around the yolk weakens, making it more difficult for the cook to separate white and yolk without the yolk breaking. Eventually the egg rots, producing smelly hydrogen sulphide from the yolk.

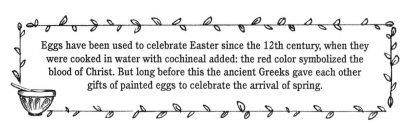

Eggs have been used to celebrate Easter since the 12th century, when they were cooked in water with cochineal added: the red color symbolized the blood of Christ. But long before this the ancient Greeks gave each other gifts of painted eggs to celebrate the arrival of spring.

WHISK EGG WHITES IN A COPPER BOWL

● ●

For a stable foam that can be whisked stiff and will not collapse, there is nothing to surpass a copper bowl. But a clean, dry container, whatever it is made of, is essential to a good result.

One of the problems of beating egg whites stiff, particularly for making meringues, is that if over-beaten they separate out into a nasty mess of lumps and liquid. What cooks of the past discovered by trial and error has now been proved in the laboratory: a reaction between conalbumin (one of the proteins in the white) and the copper prevents the foam from separating and imparts a creamy yellow color quite different from the snowy white of a foam whisked in a glass, stainless steel or ceramic bowl.

The first egg whisks were bunches of birch twigs, used in the 16th century to make 'snows' of beaten egg whites and cream, the forerunners of meringues.

Pure egg white is essential to a good result. Just a drop of yolk can reduce the volume of beaten egg white by over 60 percent; particles of oil or grease can have a less drastic effect. Salt makes whites hard to whip and decreases their stability. If you have a copper bowl, keep it spotless. Rub off any green patches of potentially harmful copper oxide with a mixture of salt and lemon juice, then wash and dry it thoroughly before use.

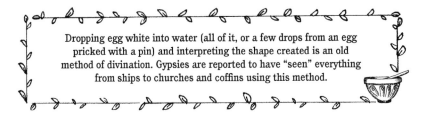

Dropping egg white into water (all of it, or a few drops from an egg pricked with a pin) and interpreting the shape created is an old method of divination. Gypsies are reported to have "seen" everything from ships to churches and coffins using this method.

IF THE SOUP IS TOO SALTY, ADD SUGAR

The trick, which works especially well for tomato soup, is also effective for gravy. The addition of sugar seems to neutralize the taste of the salt, possibly because these two basic flavors are sensed on different parts of the tongue.

Another good tip is to put a sliced potato into salty soup, then remove and discard it before serving; the vegetable will absorb a lot of the excess salt. Adding milk can help, too, but only if the soup already has milk or cream as one of its ingredients.

Soup is one of the oldest foods and for centuries was either bread soaked in broth or broth poured over bread. Only from the 1800s was it served without the bread or "sops." Soups made from game animals and birds were staples in the diet of early North American pioneers. In 1837 Miss Leslie, in her *Directions for Cookery, in its Various Branches*, advised: "Be careful to proportion the amount of water to the amount of meat. Somewhat less than a quart to a pound of meat is a good rule for common soups. Rich soups, intended for company, may have a still smaller allowance for water."

OTHER GOOD ADVICE FROM SOUP MAKERS OF THE PAST

- A good stock makes a good soup.
- Don't flavor a soup like a sauce.
- If stock for soup is fatty, heat it, then strain it through a muslin cloth that has been wrung out in cold water. The fat will solidify on the cloth.
- Clarify a soup by adding crushed eggshells to the hot liquid, then skimming them off.

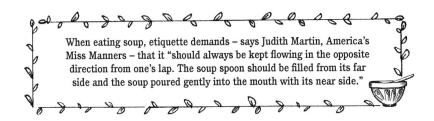

When eating soup, etiquette demands – says Judith Martin, America's Miss Manners – that it "should always be kept flowing in the opposite direction from one's lap. The soup spoon should be filled from its far side and the soup poured gently into the mouth with its near side."

TEAR LETTUCE, DON'T CHOP IT

Chopping lettuce, believe many cooks, imparts an undesirable "flavor of the knife," and quickly makes salads go limp and brown. But it is often the only way to deal satisfactorily with the ubiquitous "Icebergs" eaten by the billions each year.

Tearing lettuce is said to damage it less because it divides the leaf along the natural boundaries between the cells. In fact, left only to the air, lettuce will not (unlike basil leaves) brown quickly, however prepared, but the test comes when you add the dressing. An oil-only dressing will stick to the leaf and ooze into any breaks in its outer layer or cuticle, creating a browning reaction. Vinegar, by contrast (as with lemon juice on avocado, see "Stop Avocados Going Brown with Lemon Juice" on page 103) will stop or effectively delay the same chemical effect.

In the 17th century the French candied lettuce hearts with sugar to make the confection known as gorge d'ange *or angel's throat.*

Lettuce (*Lactuca sativa*) is named for the milky sap that is exuded from its stems and leaves. In ancient times this was associated with fertility, and the Egyptian god Min possessed a sacred bull who was fed on lettuce to maximize his potency. In the Middle Ages, however, eating lettuce was widely thought to cause sterility.

The Greek physician Hippocrates extolled the healing virtues of lettuce (though he may have been referring to wild "loose" lettuce, *L. serriola*), but it was first widely cultivated in Europe in the Roman period. In the early days of the Empire, lettuce salad was served at the end of a meal to help induce sleep. Later it became favored as an appetizer, to stimulate the palate.

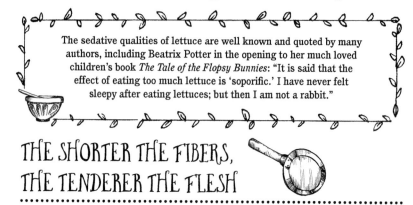

The sedative qualities of lettuce are well known and quoted by many authors, including Beatrix Potter in the opening to her much loved children's book *The Tale of the Flopsy Bunnies*: "It is said that the effect of eating too much lettuce is 'soporific.' I have never felt sleepy after eating lettuces; but then I am not a rabbit."

THE SHORTER THE FIBERS, THE TENDERER THE FLESH

A handy rule for judging the quality of the butcher's meat, although not the only important factor. The cut is critical as is, for beef especially, the length of time the meat has been hung.

Meat is muscle, made of bundles of long, thin fibers, which are supported by sheets of connective tissue containing collagen. Age and exercise toughen muscle fibers – by increasing the number of fibers in every muscle bundle – but with age also comes the deposition of fat, the "marbling" that melts in cooking and adds to meat's succulence. Animal anatomy is also significant. The muscles of the forequarters, which the animal uses more, are generally tougher and more packed with collagen than those of the rump or those near the spine and under the backbone.

Cuts such as steaks combine the advantages of being from the rump of the animal and having short fibers. Slicing meat across the grain – as in a T-bone steak or meat sliced for a stroganoff or a Chinese stir fry – helps to create short fibers that, although probably already tender, are extremely easy to chew.

Tenderness also depends on an animal's health. A well-fed creature will have plump muscle fibers packed with the carbohydrate glycogen. In the carcass this is converted into lactic acid, which tenderizes the flesh by breaking down the protein in the muscle fibers and also helps to prevent it from being infected with bacteria.

With hanging, enzymes are released which add both acidity and tenderness to the meat. You can judge a well-hung piece of beef by its deep – not bright – red color. Beef can safely be hung for up to six or even eight weeks, although today's commercial pressures make three weeks the norm.

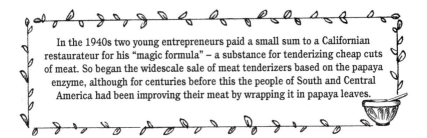

In the 1940s two young entrepreneurs paid a small sum to a Californian restaurateur for his "magic formula" – a substance for tenderizing cheap cuts of meat. So began the widescale sale of meat tenderizers based on the papaya enzyme, although for centuries before this the people of South and Central America had been improving their meat by wrapping it in papaya leaves.

DON'T STORE BANANAS IN THE FRIDGE

Because they are averse to cold. If you must refrigerate bananas, wrap them in newspaper to keep them insulated. Their skins may turn black but they should be prevented from going mushy inside.

If you want to eat or cook with bananas ripened to your taste it is best to buy them green and allow them to ripen slowly. Supermarket bananas are picked completely green and allowed to ripen somewhat during shipment. As they mature the starch in the flesh turns increasingly to the sugar glucose, which helps to alter the texture of the fruit.

When bananas are fully ripe – as you need them for mashing into a banana bread or cake mixture – the skin is deep yellow, flecked with brown spots. As they ripen they give off ethylene gas, which can help other fruit – even green tomatoes – to ripen as well. An avocado put in a lidded box with a banana should ripen overnight.

"Yes We Have No Bananas" became a popular wartime song in the food shortage days of the 1940s, although it had been written by Frank Silver and Irving Cohn long before, in 1923.

The banana's name betrays its history. It comes from a West African word, *banema*, originating from Guinea – from where the Portuguese took the fruit to the Canaries in 1402. From there banana roots arrived in America in 1516, courtesy of a Spanish missionary destined to become the Bishop of Panama.

PRICK SAUSAGE SKINS TO STOP THEM BURSTING

Pricking is a useful precaution if sausages are not the highest quality, and for any sausages to be cooked at high temperatures, but it allows the juices to leak from good sausages, reducing their succulence.

The more water there is in a sausage the more likely it is to burst when cooked. Sausages earned their nickname of "bangers" when, during the 1940s, they were so packed with water that they were likely to explode when heated. Modern sausage makers recommend no pricking and slow frying or cooking under a moderate grill to stop the skins bursting. An old method of toughening sausage skins or casings – made from animal intestines or, as Fannie Farmer called them, "prepared entrails" – was to dip the sausages in boiling water before they were cooked.

The expression 'not a sausage', which when first coined meant lack of money, relates back to cockney rhyming slang in which bangers and mash equal cash.

Many culinary regions have characteristic types of sausage that relate closely to the climate. So it is no accident that dried sausages that keep well, such as salami and chorizo, came first from warm countries such as Italy and Spain. The Frankfurter is named for Frankfurt am Main, but "hot dog" entered the vocabulary when, in 1906, the American cartoonist Tad Dorgan first depicted a sausage dog (a dachshund) served up in a bun.

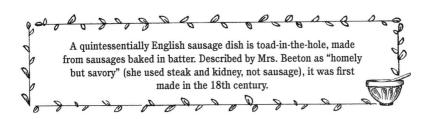

A quintessentially English sausage dish is toad-in-the-hole, made from sausages baked in batter. Described by Mrs. Beeton as "homely but savory" (she used steak and kidney, not sausage), it was first made in the 18th century.

AFTER MELON, WINE IS A FELON

Not only melon, but any sweet food, can ruin the taste of a wine. The rule for choosing wine to accompany sweet dishes is that it should be sweeter than the food.

This advice, and the mantras "dry before sweet" and "light before full," make melon a difficult ingredient to pair with wine at the start of a meal. But, if you match it with a savory accompaniment such as Parma ham, a fruity German or New Zealand white wine would be a good choice.

Dessert wines have returned to favor, especially for home entertaining, and are the perfect match for sweet food. French Sauternes, not to be confused with the sugary Spanish or Californian "Sauterne" gulped by the gallon by students in the 1960s (it was the only wine affordable and available), has a luscious intensity and is appropriate to serve with desserts

MORE WINE ADVICE
Apart from desserts, there are some other tricky tastes that need careful wine selection:

Acid foods like lemon – "acid with acid," such as a dry Graves, high in tartaric acid.
Asparagus – Sauvignon Blanc.
Curries – A dry, aromatic Pinot Gris (or just drink lager).
Artichokes – Forget wine. The chemical cynarin that artichokes contain will make any wine nastily metallic on the palate.

such as strawberries and cream. Or choose an Australian Muscat or a Tokay, which will go well with even the sweetest chocolate mousse.
In the grand houses and restaurants of 1890s America, champagne would often be served throughout a meal "with no other adjunct but bottled waters." But as the social adviser Constance Cary Harrison also remarked, "How infinitely more welcome to the habitual diner-out is a glass of good claret than indifferent champagne!"

150 Hors d'oeuvre Recipes by "Pin" Baglioni of the Embassy Club, published in 1934, includes a "special" first course in which cantaloupe melon flesh is diced and served (in the scooped-out melon halves) with a sauce made from a mixture of curry powder, ginger, port, kirsch, whipped cream, apricot purée and sugar!

SERVE WHITE WINE WITH FISH, RED WINE WITH MEAT

A helpful guide, not an unbreakable golden rule. The secret of success in matching wine with food is to think of the wine as another ingredient.

Following this logic, it makes perfect sense to enjoy an acid wine such as a Sauvignon, Reisling or Muscadet with fish in the same way that you would squeeze lemon over it. Similarly, a rich, full-bodied wine such as a Shiraz or Merlot is an excellent accompaniment to beef or game, while the acidity of a Cabernet Sauvignon makes it a perfect foil for rich roast pork.

If red is your preferred color, but fish your food, it is best to avoid wines high in tannins such as vintage Burgundies. But there are many good, light acidic reds to choose from, including young Riojas, Chiantis and Valpolicellas. For a white that will complement a meat dish, body is required, and you will get it from wines such as Pinot Gris, Chardonnay and Semillon.

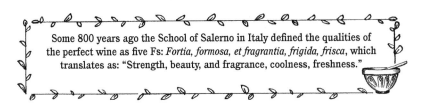

Some 800 years ago the School of Salerno in Italy defined the qualities of the perfect wine as five Fs: *Fortia, formosa, et fragrantia, frigida, frisca*, which translates as: "Strength, beauty, and fragrance, coolness, freshness."

ADD FRESH HERBS AT THE END OF COOKING, DRIED AT THE BEGINNING

An assured route to good flavor, but not advice to apply slavishly. For dishes such as casseroles a *bouquet garni* – fresh parsley, rosemary and thyme added at the beginning – is needed for depth and subtlety of taste.

Like rosemary and thyme, bay and sage have sturdy leaves that will impart flavor throughout the cooking of a dish. Herbs with more tender foliage, including fresh coriander, chives, dill, fennel, basil, mint and tarragon, are best kept until shortly before the end of cooking for their flavor to be fully appreciated (as is fresh parsley if you want its flavor to be dominant, as in parsley sauce) because when cooked for more than a few minutes their taste goes flat.

Equally, none of these delicate herbs holds its aroma well when dried, although they freeze well (ice cube trays make excellent containers). Or try making good quantities of garden mint into sauce or jelly, and turn basil into your own pesto, which will keep for at least a month in the refrigerator.

The specific aromatic notes of herbs – created from a whole spectrum of chemicals that are released when the leaves are crushed or heated – make them perfect partners for certain ingredients: mint or rosemary with lamb; fennel or dill with fish; bay with ham; sage with pork; tarragon with eggs. Fresh coriander comes into its own in chilli-based Thai curries.

ADD LEMON TO STRAWBERRY JAM TO MAKE IT SET

If you're having real trouble, you also need to add pectin, the carbohydrate – which strawberries have too little of – that makes jams and jellies set. Lemon juice helps the setting process by drawing out all the pectin that is available from the fruit.

The essential process of jam making is simple: boil the fruit with its own weight in sugar until, when a small amount is dabbed on to a cold plate, it cools to a firm consistency. While fruits like plums, currants and gooseberries contain plenty of natural pectin so jams made with them set with ease, strawberries and all but the most acid raspberries are notorious for their reluctance to set. Try boiling unpeeled lemon slices and using the resulting liquid (which contains pectin from the fruit pith) or, to ensure success, use natural pectin, which is available ready-prepared in powder or liquid form, or mixed into special preserving sugar.

Jams are relative newcomers to the kitchen cupboard, being first recorded in the 1730s, some 200 years after solid marmalades and fruit cheeses were originally made. Because they needed so much sugar to ensure a set and good keeping qualities, jams remained a luxury. As Mrs. Beeton observed: "The expense of preserving them [fruits] with sugar is a serious objection; for, except the sugar is used in considerable quantities, the success is very uncertain."

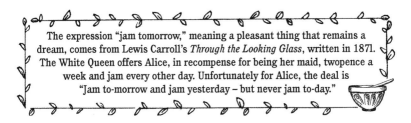

The expression "jam tomorrow," meaning a pleasant thing that remains a dream, comes from Lewis Carroll's *Through the Looking Glass*, written in 1871. The White Queen offers Alice, in recompense for being her maid, twopence a week and jam every other day. Unfortunately for Alice, the deal is "Jam to-morrow and jam yesterday – but never jam to-day."

HEALTH AND BEAUTY

Although they may have followed the advice in ancient health manuals such as the Babylonian Code of Hammurabi, written in the 18th century BC, which included instructions for the use of herbs, ancient peoples also believed illness to be the vengeance of the gods and the work of evil spirits. Such spirits were thought to be deterred by a beautifully decorated body. Early cosmetics, such as the kohl around the eyes of Egyptian women, also helped to protect them from the sun and keep diseases at bay.

As medical knowledge advanced, people found it hard to shake off their belief in the old wives' tales. By the 19th century there was a huge trade in patent medicines with secret formulas, promising cures for everything from coughs to constipation and corns. Also widely advertised were beauty products for hair and skin, and hinged appliances to replace missing limbs.

While they may not have been correct in every regard it is remarkable how many of the old cures have been discovered by modern medical science to have a sound basis, whether it is the benefits of walking or laughter, that it is wise to stay out of the sun, or that fish is indeed good for the brain.

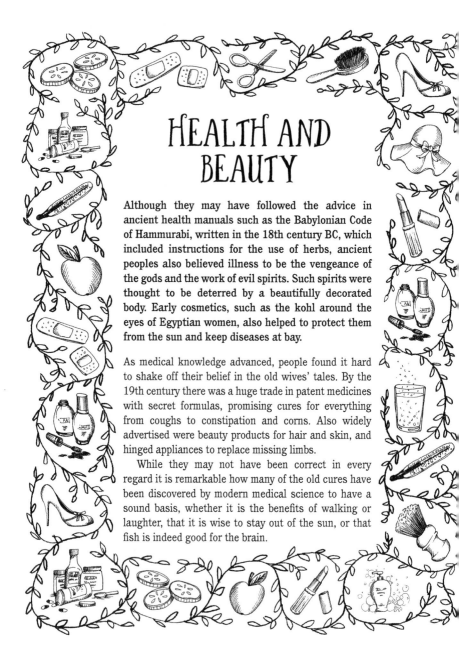

CARROTS HELP YOU SEE IN THE DARK

This saying, popular in the blackouts of World War II, when carrots were prized for their sweetness as substitutes for sugar, contains more than a grain of truth.

Carrots are a great source of beta carotene, the plant form of vitamin A, and it is this vitamin that helps to prevent night blindness by combining with the protein opsin in the retina at the back of the eye to form rhodopsin, the chemical essential for good

Carrot conserves are still prized as a delicacy in Asia – in contrast to the carrot jam eaten under mild protest in wartime Britain as a poor substitute for marmalade.

night vision. Just one carrot a day is all it takes, and unlike many other vegetables carrots are better for you cooked than raw. Cooking breaks down the plant's tough cell walls, making the vitamin A more readily available for absorption into the bloodstream.

In wartime Britain, the Ministry of Food did its best to drum up enthusiasm for carrots. Doctor Carrot, carrying his bag marked "Vit A," was pictured on the pages of recipe books promoting such delicacies as carrot puddings. These were nothing new: carrot cakes and puddings have been enjoyed throughout Europe since the Middle Ages, and recipes have been commonplace in cookbooks since the 18th and 19th centuries.

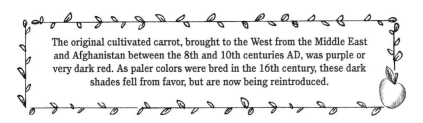

The original cultivated carrot, brought to the West from the Middle East and Afghanistan between the 8th and 10th centuries AD, was purple or very dark red. As paler colors were bred in the 16th century, these dark shades fell from favor, but are now being reintroduced.

WHITE FLECKS ON THE NAILS MEAN YOU'RE SHORT OF CALCIUM

They are more likely to be a sign that your diet is lacking zinc or possibly vitamin A, not calcium. For although calcium is needed for building strong bones and teeth, the nails are made of the fibrous protein keratin, which does not include calcium as one of its major components.

The link between calcium and white nail spots probably comes from the color association – white spots, white mineral. In superstition they are associated with receiving gifts and predicting events, as in Ben Jonson's play *The Alchemist* of 1612: "H'is a fortunate fellow, that I am sure on… And, in right way to'ward riches… I knew't, by certaine spots…on the nayle of his Mercurial [little] finger."

To get more zinc, the easy way is to take a supplement of 30 mg daily, plus 2 mg of copper, which helps the zinc to be absorbed into the body more easily. Or it could be a good excuse to eat more oysters, which are rich in zinc, as are beef, the dark meat of poultry, liver, eggs and almonds. For men, as well as boosting nail health, zinc will help pep up the sperm count.

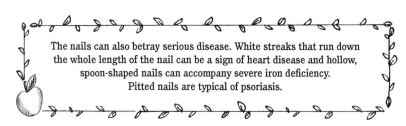

The nails can also betray serious disease. White streaks that run down the whole length of the nail can be a sign of heart disease and hollow, spoon-shaped nails can accompany severe iron deficiency. Pitted nails are typical of psoriasis.

DON'T KEEP PLANTS IN THE SICKROOM

Especially, it was said, at nighttime, for they would rob the room of vital oxygen. It is true that in darkness plants reverse their daytime activity of absorbing carbon dioxide and releasing oxygen but it would take more than a couple of vases to seriously affect the quality of the air.

Modern nurses have far greater concerns than removing plants from hospital wards at night, and plants and flowers are banned from hospital wards as potential carriers of antibiotic-resistant bugs. However our grandparents made much of the sickroom, which was

To prevent disturbing patients with unnecessary noise, maids were taught to use a gloved hand for putting coals on the fire, or to wrap lumps of fuel in newspaper.

entirely understandable in an era before the advanced antibiotics and inoculations that now cure or prevent so many illnesses.

The air of the sickroom was also likely to be polluted – at least in winter – by the fumes from a coal fire. However it was recommended that, except for patients suffering from chest and kidney complaints, the windows were "opened wide after the action of the bowels."

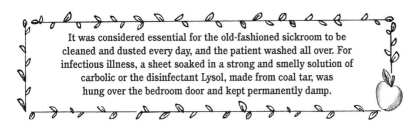

It was considered essential for the old-fashioned sickroom to be cleaned and dusted every day, and the patient washed all over. For infectious illness, a sheet soaked in a strong and smelly solution of carbolic or the disinfectant Lysol, made from coal tar, was hung over the bedroom door and kept permanently damp.

FRESHEN GARLIC BREATH BY CHEWING PARSLEY

The cook's favorite garnish is also one of the herbalist's traditional remedies for bad breath. Parsley stalks, rather than the leaves, will have the best effect, because they contain more of the plant's volatile oils.

Garlic is so potent on the breath because it is packed full of pungent sulfur-containing oils. These are carried in the blood to the lungs, released and breathed out through the mouth. In addition, smelly substances including hydrogen sulphide – the gas with the smell of bad eggs – are made from food remains by bacteria that live between the papillae, the tiny lobes in the tongue. Brushing or scraping your tongue when you brush your teeth are ways of keeping these bacteria at bay.

Not sure whether your breath is offensive? An old-fashioned test is to lick the back of your hand, let it dry for a few seconds and sniff it. If it smells bad, then so does your breath.

Like other natural breath fresheners such as aniseed and peppermint, parsley will only mask offensive odors from foods like garlic and onions, or from drinking too much wine or beer, and will not cure the underlying effects of halitosis. If bad breath persists in the absence of garlic and its sulfurous relatives, it may be your teeth or gums that are the problem, or a persistent digestive ailment – for which parsley itself is a long-used herbal remedy.

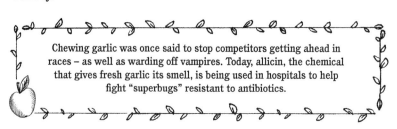

Chewing garlic was once said to stop competitors getting ahead in races – as well as warding off vampires. Today, allicin, the chemical that gives fresh garlic its smell, is being used in hospitals to help fight "superbugs" resistant to antibiotics.

SOOTHE TIRED EYES WITH CUCUMBER

The coolness of cucumber slices on closed eyelids is undoubtedly relaxing, but lying down with your contact lenses out and your eyes shut is probably as good for you as the vegetable you put on them.

The eyes get tired when you stare repeatedly at the computer screen or the pages of a book because the small muscles that control the shape of the lens and assist with focusing become fatigued. Your eyes can also get dry if you don't blink enough – blinking helpfully spreads lubricating fluid, the tear film, across the front of the eyeball. Central heating and air conditioning, which sap the air of humidity, add to the problem, but persistently tired eyes need the attention of the optician to rule out any serious underlying condition.

Cucumbers were grown and eaten by the Greeks and Romans and were esteemed by Nicholas Culpeper, who wrote in **The English Physician Enlarged** *(1653): "The face being washed with their juice cleanses the skin."*

The eye bath was essential to the Victorian medical cabinet and washing the eyes with a salt water solution was a popular remedy. In the 1920s and 1930s the pharmacist would have made up a weak solution of zinc sulfate as a cure for tired eyes. This was the recommended routine for using the eye bath: "It is filled with lotion and the patient bends forward the head and applies the edge of the bath firmly around the eye. He then throws his head back and opens the eye widely. The lotion is kept in contact with the eye for a minute or two. The cleansing may be facilitated by opening and closing the eye several times…"

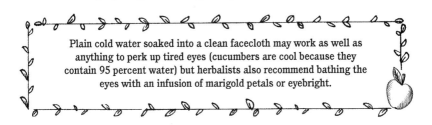

Plain cold water soaked into a clean facecloth may work as well as anything to perk up tired eyes (cucumbers are cool because they contain 95 percent water) but herbalists also recommend bathing the eyes with an infusion of marigold petals or eyebright.

ROSEHIP SYRUP KEEPS COLDS AT BAY

This may be effective if you believe that mega doses of vitamin C are the best way to control the cold virus. Weight for weight, rosehips gathered from the dog rose (*Rosa canina*) actually contain over 20 percent more vitamin C than oranges.

The idea of averting colds with doses of up to 10 grams a day of vitamin C was first advocated by the American Nobel laureate Linus Pauling in 1970. Counter to this, the latest research suggests that vitamin C reduces the duration of the symptoms rather than actually stopping a cold from occurring in the first instance. The other bad news is that there is virtually nothing that can stop the cold virus. But it's worth avoiding anyone who has just caught a cold, as the first three days of the illness are when a person is at their most infectious.

Even if it doesn't stop a cold, the vitamin C in rosehip syrup has lots of other health advantages. It fights the damage caused by "free radicals" – unstable oxygen molecules – especially inside body cells, and in doing so helps to protect against cancer and heart disease.

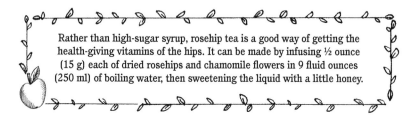

Rather than high-sugar syrup, rosehip tea is a good way of getting the health-giving vitamins of the hips. It can be made by infusing ½ ounce (15 g) each of dried rosehips and chamomile flowers in 9 fluid ounces (250 ml) of boiling water, then sweetening the liquid with a little honey.

ALWAYS CUT TOENAILS STRAIGHT ACROSS

Still the best way of preventing ingrowing toenails, this is most easily done after a bath or swim when the nails are soft.

When you cut into the sides of a big toenail, the "nail folds" (the skin around the nail) can become swollen, and often painful and infected. Wearing shoes that are too tight can have the same effect – that is, to make the nail dig into the puffed-up skin. Despite the pain, it was known for schoolboys in the 1950s to inflict the problem on themselves to avoid compulsory games and cross-country runs.

At the first sign of an ingrowing toenail, the old-fashioned, painful treatment was to soak the nail in hot water for 10 minutes then raise the corner of the nail and press a piece of cotton wool under it. Today, antibiotics will most likely be prescribed to treat the infection, but scrupulous attention to hygiene is vital. In severe cases, surgery is necessary to remove part of the nail base, from which it grows.

NAIL CUTTING DAYS
For the superstitious, the day of the week on which you cut your nails is crucial, as in this old rhyme:

Cut them on Monday,
you cut them for health,
Cut them on Tuesday,
you cut them for wealth,
Cut them on Wednesday,
you cut them for news,
Cut them on Thursday,
a new pair of shoes,

Cut them on Friday,
you cut them for sorrow,
Cut them on Saturday,
you see your true love tomorrow,
Cut them on Sunday,
your safety seek,
The Devil will have you
the rest of the week.

FISH IS GOOD FOR THE BRAIN

••

It is, and just as good for your heart – especially oily fish like salmon, mackerel and herrings. Eating fish won't make you a genius, but will help to keep your whole nervous system in good shape.

W hat oily fish does best for the brain is to protect it from strokes – interruptions to the blood supply, often caused by blood clots, which kill brain cells and leave victims with anything from a slight paralysis on one side of the body to total loss of both memory and speech. The most effective substances in fish are omega-3 fatty acids, which help to keep the arteries clear. They may also help lift depression and even reduce the risk of dementia.

Latest research suggests that the fatty acids in fish may help recovery from chronic fatigue syndrome by effecting 'repairs' in the brain.

All fish benefit the nervous system by supplying good quantities of vitamin B12, and the oily varieties also provide vitamin A (vital for good eyesight) and vitamin D (for strong bones). And everyone can get at least a third of the protein they need each day by eating just 3½ ounces (100 g) of any fish.

A swallowed fishbone can scratch the throat, making it feel as though it is stuck. If a bone is truly stuck, eating poorly chewed bread is a good way of dislodging it. Sipping neat lemon juice may help dissolve a small bone, but one that can't be shifted needs medical attention.

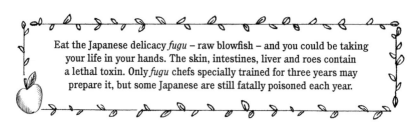

Eat the Japanese delicacy *fugu* – raw blowfish – and you could be taking your life in your hands. The skin, intestines, liver and roes contain a lethal toxin. Only *fugu* chefs specially trained for three years may prepare it, but some Japanese are still fatally poisoned each year.

TREAT A NETTLE STING WITH A DOCK LEAF

Handily, the stinger and its antidote are often found growing near each other, and a bruised dock leaf has been known for generations as the best emergency treatment. It is said to work particularly well if you also chant the rhyme "Nettle out, dock in, dock remove the nettle sting."

The broad-leaved dock (*Rumex obtusifolius*) creates its soothing effect because its leaves are rich in oxalates. These chemicals cool the skin, which becomes inflamed when pierced by the minute tips of the stinging hairs on the stinging nettle (*Urtica dioica*). The tips snap off and lodge in the skin when the leaf or stem is touched; here they release their poisonous load. Among them is histamine, the chief culprit in causing inflammation.

The best way of avoiding stings is to grip a nettle tightly so that the tips of the hairs break off before they have a chance of entering the skin. "Grasping the nettle" has been synonymous with bravery since the 17th century.

The best home treatment for nettle stings is to apply an ice pack, a cool compress soaked in bicarbonate of soda solution, or old-fashioned calamine lotion. If a severe reaction flares up, in which the face swells and breathing becomes labored or difficult, call for emergency medical help.

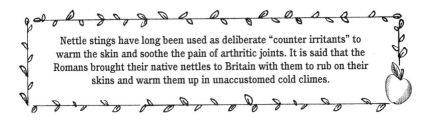

Nettle stings have long been used as deliberate "counter irritants" to warm the skin and soothe the pain of arthritic joints. It is said that the Romans brought their native nettles to Britain with them to rub on their skins and warm them up in unaccustomed cold climes.

ADAM'S ALE IS THE BEST BREW

That is water, the world's first drink, named from the first man, and the fluid vital to life. Its importance is shown in its symbolic use in Christian baptism, named from the Greek *baptizein*, meaning "to dip in water."

The adult body, which itself is about 60 percent water, needs water for keeping all its parts well lubricated and for essential tasks such as digestion. And since water is continuously expelled as we breathe, as well as in the other processes of living, it needs to be constantly replaced.

Luckily, most food is also water-rich (we get about a quarter of all the water we need from what we eat, and most of all from fruit and vegetables), but the experts reckon that we should all drink around 4½ pints (2 liters) of water a day just to keep the system topped up, and more if we exercise vigorously and lose water in sweat. Dehydration makes you feel headachy, sluggish and lethargic and can be a precipitating factor in conditions such as kidney stones and urinary infections. To see if you're drinking enough water, do the "urine test." It should be pale and clear like a Muscadet wine, not dark in color.

The first water drawn from a well on New Year's Day was thought, in country districts, to endow good fortune if sprinkled on passers-by. If drunk it was also believed to bring beauty and wealth.

The health-giving properties of the water at spa towns has been long appreciated. Bath, which was developed by the Romans, became a medieval destination for pilgrims in search of healing cures. In Europe, places such as Baden-Baden in Germany and Spa in Belgium became fashionable places to: "take the waters" from the 16th century.

As for today's water, hard high-mineral tap water is healthier than soft. And all tap water, as long as it is guaranteed free from bacterial contamination, is as good for you (and your pocket) as bottled water, which can be high in sodium.

COLD HANDS, WARM HEART

A saying true for the body, if not the soul. When we get cold the circulation in our extremities closes down to protect the inner organs – the heart included – which is why it is possible to survive severe frostbite in both hands and feet.

Like other warm-blooded animals, the bodies of humans are tuned to maintain a constant temperature – in our case 98.4°F (37°C). As soon as our internal sensors register that we are getting cold, our self-protective mechanisms go into action. First we get goose bumps as our hair stands on end in an attempt to improve body insulation. Then we shiver,

If cold hands mean a warm heart, a moist hand is said to betray an amorous nature.

generating warmth through muscle movement. Simultaneously, blood is diverted to the body's core, shielding key organs from potentially fatal blood clots and strokes.

Apart from wearing gloves, exercise to get the circulation going is a good way of keeping the hands warm. Or it can be pepped up with ginger, a spice long renowned for dilating the blood vessels and stimulating the circulation; it tastes especially good mixed with lemon, honey and hot water.

Servants such as scullery maids, with their hands constantly in water, suffered greatly from raw, chapped hands. But in the early 20th century they were advised that: "Vigorous scrubbing with a soft nailbrush when washing stimulates the circulation… For chapped hands, clarified mutton fat, perfumed to liking, is a simple but efficacious remedy."

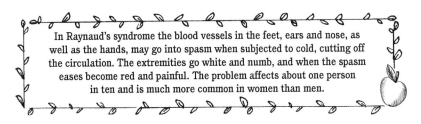

In Raynaud's syndrome the blood vessels in the feet, ears and nose, as well as the hands, may go into spasm when subjected to cold, cutting off the circulation. The extremities go white and numb, and when the spasm eases become red and painful. The problem affects about one person in ten and is much more common in women than men.

PALE IS BEAUTIFUL

Especially if you want to avoid sunburn and, ultimately, skin cancer. Until the 1920s, when the suntan first became fashionable, any woman who considered herself a "lady" would do everything possible to avoid having a reddened or tanned skin like that of a farmworker.

W hen exposed to the sun the skin reacts by producing extra amounts of the dark, protective substance melanin, but fair skins can easily become burned well before this happens. Cells are probably triggered to become cancerous by the sun's UVA and UVB rays, especially if the skin has been overexposed to them during childhood.

Get a hat. Headwear with a brim 4 inches (10 cm) wide can cut your risk of skin cancer by up to 40 percent.

Avoiding the sun between 11:00 a.m. and 3:00 p.m., covering up and using a sunscreen with a high protection factor (30 plus, or a total block in the case of fair skin) are the proven ways to cut the risk. Do not forget vulnerable spots such as the lips and the backs of the knees and, if you do burn, apply calamine lotion or aloe vera to help cool the skin and speed healing.

When bicycling became the vogue in the late 19th century, *Cycling Hints for Ladies* suggested: "A veil [worn over a hat]…as a protection against flies, and to conceal a flushed face," and "To avoid sunburn, if the skin is delicate, a lady should, before starting, rub glycerine in. If the skin is already affected by the sun, either milk or lemon juice, glycerine or cucumber, or sulpholine lotion is very useful."

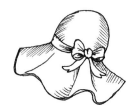

HIGH HEELS GIVE YOU BACKACHE

• •

They can, because they shift your center of gravity and in doing so put extra strain on the spine. But for many women there is no confidence booster to beat the stiletto heel.

High heels put the spine out of kilter by transferring the weight forwards from the heels (which bear, together with the hips and backbone, most of the body's weight) to the toes. Although it helps to have an ankle support to prevent the toes from "clawing" as they try to keep the shoe on the foot, high heels affect some people more adversely than others. Trouble is most likely if the extra height adds an exaggerated curve to your lower spine, making you hollow-backed.

A heel is a man devoid of any sense of honor or decency. The expression is of American origin.

If worn every day of the week, high heels can exacerbate bunions as well as backache, but sometimes only a high heel will do. Late Victorian women were advised that when "the heel is placed exactly in the right spot…and the slipper fits snugly and comfortably…it is no more injurious to wear under these conditions than any other well fitting shoe, and gives a certain elasticity to the carriage of the graceful woman that a flat shoe never does."

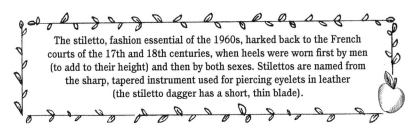

The stiletto, fashion essential of the 1960s, harked back to the French courts of the 17th and 18th centuries, when heels were worn first by men (to add to their height) and then by both sexes. Stilettos are named from the sharp, tapered instrument used for piercing eyelets in leather (the stiletto dagger has a short, thin blade).

KEEP HAIR A NATURAL BLOND WITH CHAMOMILE

••

An age-old, mild and effective treatment that gives a much more natural look than "raw" peroxide. The favorite herb of Elizabethan gardens, chamomile, also spelled camomile, has a wide range of medicinal uses.

The "Beauty Culture" section of the 1933 *News Chronicle Housewife's Handy Book* strongly recommends chamomile for blonds: "Simmer a handful of camomile flowers in a pint of water. Strain through fine muslin and apply to the hair with a small brush, parting hair so that every part is wetted. Leave for twelve minutes or so, and rinse away with warm, soft water."

The same book is heartily critical of the "peroxide blonde": "The woman who uses plain peroxide for her hair does a very foolish thing, apart from the fact that peroxide produces such a metallic and unnatural shade that a 'peroxide blonde' has become a phrase that expresses the absolutely artificial and undesirable."

Chamomile comes in many varieties including *Chamaemelum nobile*, the lawn species, but it is German chamomile (*Matricaria recutita*) that has been most widely used for centuries to treat everything from digestive disorders and insomnia to fungal skin infections, inflamed gums, sinusitis and asthma. A chamomile poultice was a common country remedy for soothing sprains and strains.

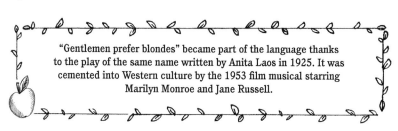

"Gentlemen prefer blondes" became part of the language thanks to the play of the same name written by Anita Laos in 1925. It was cemented into Western culture by the 1953 film musical starring Marilyn Monroe and Jane Russell.

PUT VINEGAR ON A WASP STING

Or rub it with a cut onion, great-grandmother would have said. Unlike a bee, which leaves its sting in the skin (it needs carefully removing with tweezers), the wasp injects its poison then flies off to sting again.

The best wasp sting remedies – lemon juice is another – neutralize the alkalinity of the sting. An ice pack will help calm any swelling. It was once thought that the toxin could travel to and poison the heart. In fact what can be fatal following both wasp and bee stings is anaphylaxis, an extreme allergic reaction in which the air passages swell up and breathing is fatally impaired as a result.

In late summer, wasps in orchards were traditionally trapped in jars filled with beer or sugared water hung in the trees. Enticed to drink, the insects would drown. In the past sulfur was used to fumigate wasps' nests, but a more humane solution is to leave it until the end of the season, when the colony will disappear anyway, then block off the hole or crevice in which it formed.

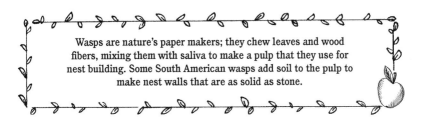

Wasps are nature's paper makers; they chew leaves and wood fibers, mixing them with saliva to make a pulp that they use for nest building. Some South American wasps add soil to the pulp to make nest walls that are as solid as stone.

COUGHS AND SNEEZES SPREAD DISEASES

"Trap the germs in your handkerchief." So ran the slogan on the British 1942 wartime poster, when food and fuel were scarce and good health at a premium. And beware of touching anything – microbes can easily spread on everything from fingers to doorknobs and pieces of paper.

The germs – bacteria and viruses – that cause disease are forced from the body at high speed in coughs and sneezes, which makes these a simple and effective way for germs to spread from person to person. But the diseases that make us sneeze and splutter, especially colds and flu, are also spread by touch, so as well as avoiding the newly infectious, deter infection by washing your hands, especially if you've been handed anything by someone with a cold. If you can, avoid touching your mouth or nose until you have done so.

According to Pliny in his **Natural History** *of AD 77, the first wasp of the year, caught and attached under a patient's chin, would cure a fever.*

The good handkerchief was still much prized when *The House and Home Practical Book* of 1896 declared: "When it comes to certain accessories of the toilet, notably handkerchiefs, every American woman has cause to regret that she was not born in Paris. The French handkerchiefs are so superior in texture, in ornamentation and so maddeningly cheap in comparison." However, it continued, "so called fancy handkerchiefs, made of chiffon are…not to be recommended…its adoption as an ornament is not to be sanctioned…"

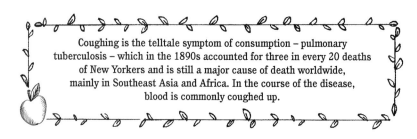

Coughing is the telltale symptom of consumption – pulmonary tuberculosis – which in the 1890s accounted for three in every 20 deaths of New Yorkers and is still a major cause of death worldwide, mainly in Southeast Asia and Africa. In the course of the disease, blood is commonly coughed up.

EATING YOGURT MAKES YOU LIVE LONGER

A saying that owes its origins to the fact that Georgia and the Smolyan region of Bulgaria, where yogurt is a staple part of the diet, boast large numbers of centenarians. Whether it adds to your lifespan or not, yogurt has some undoubted health benefits.

Whether made from the milk of cows, sheep, goats, camels or even yaks, all yogurt is made by the action of bacteria, *Lactobacillus bulgaricus* and *Streptococcus thermophiles*; these produce lactic acid that sours, curdles and thickens the milk. In the Caucasian mountains, yeasts are added to make a type of yogurt called *kefir*, which is slightly alcoholic and has a thick, frothy head like beer.

To cool the palate when eating foods hot with chilli, yogurt works much better than water. In Indian cuisine it is mixed with cucumber and mint to make raita.

When you eat "live" yogurt the bacteria it contains add to the natural "flora" of the digestive system. Here they not only hamper the multiplication of other micro-organisms, including *E. coli* and the yeast *Candida albicans*, but produce a range of chemicals that enhance the absorption of nutrients. Probiotic yogurts, containing the bacteria *Lactobacillus casei*, are believed to help protect against cancer by boosting the immune system.

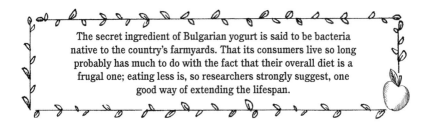

The secret ingredient of Bulgarian yogurt is said to be bacteria native to the country's farmyards. That its consumers live so long probably has much to do with the fact that their overall diet is a frugal one; eating less is, so researchers strongly suggest, one good way of extending the lifespan.

SLEEPING ON YOUR BACK MAKES YOU SNORE

Yes it does, but there are other reasons too, such as having a cold that blocks up your nose. Nighttime nuisance aside, one type of snoring can lead to a life-threatening lack of oxygen.

"There ain't no way," said the American novelist Mark Twain in *Tom Sawyer Abroad* (1894), "to find out why a snorer can't hear himself snore." This is a sentiment shared by many a wife whose husband is oblivious to night time noise reaching 80 decibels (the maximum set by Vancouver traffic bylaws) or more; this is far from a sexist observation since serious male snorers far outnumber female ones.

To stop snoring, force yourself to sleep on your side, not your back. Make a pocket in the back of your pyjamas or nightdress and insert a tennis ball or large marble.

Snoring is the sound of the soft tissues of the throat vibrating. It happens when air pushed out from the lungs rushes through constricted passages – such as when you lie on your back and your tongue lolls towards your throat, partially blocking it. Other factors come into play, too. If you're overweight, fatty tissue can narrow your airways, and the relaxing effect of alcohol makes them loose and vibratory.

Snoring becomes dangerous when the amount of oxygen getting to the lungs is seriously impaired. This is the condition called sleep apnea, which needs medical attention and is typified by loud, frequent and irregular snoring with interruptions that sound as if the snorer has stopped breathing.

CURE A HANGOVER WITH THE "HAIR OF THE DOG THAT BIT YOU"

In other words another drink. This is effective, but only because it puts recovery on hold. Popular cures for the thumping head and sandpaper mouth have been invented in every age.

There are good reasons why alcohol produces hangovers. It causes dehydration; it reduces blood sugar levels; when processed by the liver it produces toxic by-products; and it contains chemicals, including methanol, that contaminate the system. Alcohol in drinks comes in two sorts, ethanol and methanol, which the liver tackles in that order. When it starts on the methanol it begins to produce its dire effects, releasing formic acid into the system. Having another drink puts the liver back into ethanol-processing mode, delaying the methanol effect.

Line your stomach; alcohol is absorbed more slowly if you eat before you drink.

Anything that raises blood sugar levels and adds water will help a hangover. This could be anything from a fatty bacon sandwich downed with large quantities of water or tea to paracetemol (acetaminophin) swallowed with a mashed banana and a pint of sweetened orange juice. A remedy from the 1880s onwards was John Pemberton's tonic (destined to become Coca Cola) containing cocaine, caffeine and alcohol dissolved in caramel syrup and diluted with carbonated water.

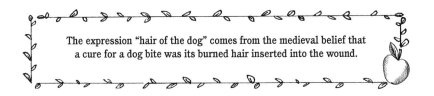

The expression "hair of the dog" comes from the medieval belief that a cure for a dog bite was its burned hair inserted into the wound.

CARE BRINGS GRAY HAIR

A saying that originates from the way in which the hair can apparently turn gray overnight, but whether it begins when you're 30 or 60, gray hair is usually an inevitable family inheritance.

The prisoner in Byron's poem "The Prisoner of Chillon" (1816) begins his story by asserting:

My hair is gray, but not with years,
Nor grew it white
In a single night,
As men's have grown from sudden fears.

In fact, hair goes gray when pigment-producing cells in the hair follicles stop making melanin, the substance that gives hair its color. By the time you see they are gray the hairs are already dead, so there's no point in pulling them out in the hope of something better! A severe shock or illness can make hair fall out, giving the impression that the hair has suddenly gone gray and, when it grows back, it can be paler.

Plants, particularly mature leaves of henna, *Lawsonia inermia*, have been used for at least 5,000 years to color the hair – and also for ceremonial decoration of the hands and nails. Some boiling water poured over a couple of handfuls of dried cornflowers (*Centaurea cyanus*), infused for a few hours and strained, makes a traditional herbal rinse that tints gray hair a delicate blue.

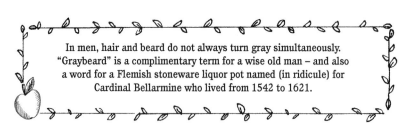

In men, hair and beard do not always turn gray simultaneously. "Graybeard" is a complimentary term for a wise old man – and also a word for a Flemish stoneware liquor pot named (in ridicule) for Cardinal Bellarmine who lived from 1542 to 1621.

AN APPLE A DAY KEEPS THE DOCTOR AWAY

A 19th-century saying that may have arisen because no other fruit is cultivated and eaten in more countries of the world. Like other fruit, apples do you good because, among other things, they are rich in vitamins and fiber.

Apples promote a healthy circulation and immune system because they contain vitamin C and (in their skins) flavonoids, both antioxidants that also help keep arteries clear of clogging cholesterol. The soluble fiber they contain helps to cure constipation and their plant sugar fructose, metabolized more slowly than glucose, provides sustained energy. To make a "cooling drink for sick persons," *Enquire Within* in the 1890s recommended "a tart apple well baked and mashed, on which pour a pint of boiling water. Beat up, cool and strain. Add sugar if desired."

That a favored person is the "apple of your eye" comes from Psalm 17: "Guard me like the apple of your eye; hide me in the shadow of your wings, from the wicked who do me violence…"

But an apple a day also "keeps the dentist in pay." For although eating a crunchy apple scrapes plaque-forming bacteria off the teeth, acids in the fruit pulp soften tooth enamel while the sugars provide ready sustenance for the microbes of decay.

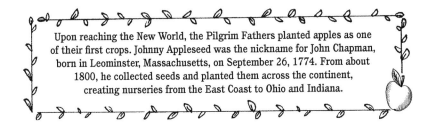

Upon reaching the New World, the Pilgrim Fathers planted apples as one of their first crops. Johnny Appleseed was the nickname for John Chapman, born in Leominster, Massachusetts, on September 26, 1774. From about 1800, he collected seeds and planted them across the continent, creating nurseries from the East Coast to Ohio and Indiana.

FATS MAKE YOU FAT

Because fats are more packed with calories than other foods, eating them to excess can help pile on the pounds. But when food was scarce, plumpness was a sign of affluence and, in women like those depicted by the Flemish painter Sir Peter Paul Rubens in "The Three Graces" (1639), a mark of sensuality.

We enjoy eating fats because they not only give food a good flavor but impart a smooth texture that makes it slip down easily – the crucial difference between dry bread and bread and butter, or old-fashioned bread and dripping (the solidified fat from a roast joint). And no matter whether they are "good" unsaturated fats, like olive oil, or "bad" saturated fats from animal products (the ones linked to heart disease), all pure fats supply us with about 250 kilocalories per ounce (9 calories per gram). By comparison, even pure carbohydrate such as sugar contains only about 111 calories per ounce (4 calories per gram).

Weight Watchers was founded in 1961 by Jean Nidetch, an overweight New York City housewife who initially formed a support group with her friends for mutual advice and encouragement.

When it comes to weight the simple truth is that if you take in more calories than you burn then your body stores the excess as fat. That obesity is a problem today is exemplified by the fact that while in 1900 Americans obtained on average 30 percent of their daily calories from fat, a century later it was at least 40 percent – between six and eight times as much as the body needs for essential jobs such as cell maintenance and repair.

LAUGHTER IS THE BEST MEDICINE

What grandmother knew by instinct, science confirms. Laughter boosts immunity, stimulates the brain and reduces stress. The old jokes are, it seems, still the best, and it is said that no man ever distinguished himself who could not bear to be laughed at.

Laughing is so good for you that laughter therapy is fast being developed as a form of treatment for people with chronic and long-term illnesses such as diabetes, multiple sclerosis, myalgic encephalomyelitis and cancer. Laughter increases the production of mood-enhancing endorphins, lowers blood levels of the stress hormone cortisol and improves immune system performance.

According to the old proverb, if you laugh before breakfast you will cry before supper.

When we laugh we not only exercise our lungs and vocal cords but also unlock our inhibitions, making it easy to mock the plights of characters such as the puppets Punch and Judy. Punch who, though wicked, manages to escape from the Devil (symbolized by the crocodile) but not from his nagging wife, is based on the Italian character Pulcinello from the 16th-century *commedia dell'arte*.

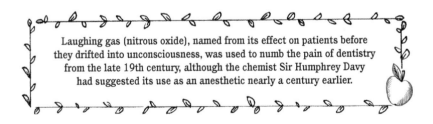

Laughing gas (nitrous oxide), named from its effect on patients before they drifted into unconsciousness, was used to numb the pain of dentistry from the late 19th century, although the chemist Sir Humphrey Davy had suggested its use as an anesthetic nearly a century earlier.

YOU SHOULD BREAKFAST LIKE A KING...
AND DINE LIKE A PAUPER

The first meal of the day, the end of the night's "fast," is the chance to replenish energy supplies. And there is some evidence that people who eat a good breakfast have less trouble controlling their weight than those who don't.

In studies of eating behavior, researchers discovered that many (but not all) thin folks who eat breakfast consume fewer calories for the rest of the day than those who do not and, as a bonus, find it easier to stick to a calorie-controlled diet. Other trials confirm that high-fiber foods eaten early in the day are effective at taming hunger and that giving children wholewheat cereal or porridge for breakfast seems to be a good way of preventing them from gaining excess weight.

Kedgeree – a curried dish of smoked fish, rice and hard boiled eggs – was a popular import to Britain in the days of the Raj. The original breakfast dish khichri, *made from mung beans and rice, has been made and enjoyed for centuries.*

On the farm, milk and eggs, direct from dairy and henhouse, were the natural, readily available breakfast choices. Over the years other foods became breakfast favorites; in the grand 19th-century home bacon, kidneys (often devilled), kippers, kedgeree, sausages, tomatoes and mushrooms would be on offer for guests, served in the dining room or a separate breakfast room.

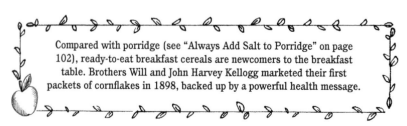

Compared with porridge (see "Always Add Salt to Porridge" on page 102), ready-to-eat breakfast cereals are newcomers to the breakfast table. Brothers Will and John Harvey Kellogg marketed their first packets of cornflakes in 1898, backed up by a powerful health message.

STRESS GIVES YOU ULCERS
• •

Up to a point, but for most people with ulcers in the stomach or
duodenum – and in the mouth – the primary cause is infection. But
stress, because it can lower your immunity, doesn't help.

In the intestine, it is the bacterium *Helicobacter (H.) pylori* that is the
culprit in forming ulcers. It is estimated that half the population
harbor it, probably from childhood, although only a fifth of these actually
develop ulcers. In a peptic
ulcer, which can affect the
esophagus, stomach or
duodenum, the lining of the
intestine is attacked and
eroded by acid juices.
Antibiotics, combined with

*Although the ulcer-prone are advised to
avoid irritants such as tobacco smoke,
alcohol and spices, they no longer face the
old treatments of bed rest, bland food and
"free administration of bismuth and alkalis."*

drugs to inhibit acid production – or to neutralize it, once secreted – are the
conventional treatments for peptic ulcers, but there are many traditional
remedies. These include licorice root, which increases the secretion of the
protective, sticky substance mucin in the gut, and "miraculous" mastic gum,
which has been used to treat digestive complaints for over 3,000 years and
is produced from the tree *Pistachia lentiscus*, which grows exclusively on
the Greek island of Chios. The bonus of mastic gum is that it also deals a
knockout blow to the *Herpes simplex* viruses that cause mouth ulcers and
cold sores.

NANNY KNOWS BEST

Long gone is the era when children were "seen but not heard," but there is still much to be admired – and much that is still true – in old-fashioned childcare advice. However there are few modern parents who would, or could, insist on their offspring chewing each mouthful 20 times or always sleeping with the window open.

Before effective medicines and inoculations were available to treat and ward off diseases, and before the basics of a healthy diet were understood, childhood was hazardous. Survival would certainly have taken the upper hand over etiquette until the 15th century when *The Babees' Book* of manners, including advice on cleanliness and table manners, was published.

Until the early 20th century the children of the wealthy were raised by nannies and governesses but, following World War I, many mothers found themselves without home helps. Early childcare manuals such as Sir Frederick Truby King's *Feeding and Care of Baby* (1928) advocated regimes of timed feeds and strict discipline – a stark contrast with today's relaxed attitudes, fostered by books like Benjamin Spock's *Baby and Child Care*, published in 1946 when the "baby boom" was in full swing.

SIT UP STRAIGHT

With "stand up straight," this is one of the cardinal rules of good posture, because sitting and standing tall not only help to strengthen the back but also improve self-confidence.

Sitting and standing up straight are good for the back because they set the shoulders and spine in correct alignment with the hips – the joints that bear the bulk of the body's weight. They also help to tone up the abdominal muscles, which although they do not make contact with the backbone, assist the muscles that do so, and keep the internal organs well girdled.

Good posture was a must for the carefully reared child of the 19th century. "Nothing," says a guide to mothers of the 1890s, "can be worse for a weak back than sitting forward in a heap." Even until the 1960s, girls' schools encouraged perfect deportment with prizes for excellence and regular exercises such as walking while balancing a heavy book on the head. For today's children, books carried in a heavy rucksack are more likely to be a problem, especially if the bag is hung on one shoulder, which risks setting up back problems for later life.

The spine is made up of 24 bones or vertebrae. Between the vertebrae are the fibrous discs that act as shock absorbers, which can cause problems when they slip out of position.

The Alexander technique is based on the principle that improved posture benefits the entire body and helps cure problems such as persistent headaches. Devised by the Australian actor Frederick Matthias Alexander in the late 19th century, after he began to lose his voice on stage, it teaches people how to "stand tall" as if their heads are attached to the ceiling by a piece of string.

EAT YOUR CRUSTS - THEY'LL MAKE YOUR HAIR CURL

Not true, but the fiction was understandable when crusts were hard, food was too precious to be wasted and crusts were oven baked for teething babies, and when straight hair was considered plain and dull.

Even when bobs came into fashion in the 1920s, curls were still desirable, and only with Vidal Sassoon's geometric cuts of the 1960s did they finally go "out." Curling the hair could be a messy, often painful business.

At polite afternoon tea, which became the height of fashion from the mid 19th century until after World War II, cucumber sandwiches were always served with the crusts removed.

Throughout the ancient Near East, women coated their hair in wet clay, let it dry and combed out their tresses into waves. The ringlets of well-to-do Greek women were created using curling tongs, a device "re-invented" in the 1870s by the Parisian hairdresser Marcel Grateau to create the popular "Marcel wave."

Rags and metal curlers were popular too, often left in overnight or even all day under a headscarf. The first permanent waves, introduced in London in 1906, involved using borax paste and heavy brass curlers that had to be left in the hair for six hours. But the perm caught on, and in the early days of commercial television, classic advertising slogans for home perms (based on the cold perm of 1945) included "Which twin has the Toni?" and "Friday night is Amami night."

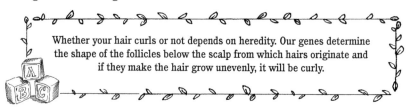

Whether your hair curls or not depends on heredity. Our genes determine the shape of the follicles below the scalp from which hairs originate and if they make the hair grow unevenly, it will be curly.

CHEW EACH MOUTHFUL TWENTY TIMES
••

Even if you stop well before the twentieth, there are good reasons for everyone to chew their food thoroughly. Apart from aiding digestion, and appreciating the full taste of each mouthful, it is possible that eating slowly can actually help you to control your weight.

Don't bolt your food" was, and is, a perpetual plea from parents to children, worried that – good table manners aside – fast eating would lead to a painful bout of stomach ache. In fact the rush of acid and enzymes that pours into the stomach when food enters, added to its muscular churning, makes it well able to cope with large pieces of food.

What you miss when you eat fast is the taste of food. As you chew, food mixes with saliva in which its chemical molecules dissolve. These then stimulate five sorts of taste buds on the tongue – for sweet, sour, salt, bitter and umami (a savory taste similar to that of monosodium glutamate typical of Chinese cooking). As a result messages are sent to the brain that are interpreted as anything from Camembert cheese to chocolate ice cream. Chewing also starts off digestion; saliva contains the enzyme amylase that begins the process of carbohydrate breakdown.

Of the five basic tastes, our tongues are most sensitive to bitterness. Because so many poisonous substances taste bitter, this is thought to have evolved as an inbuilt defense mechanism.

As the stomach fills up, its muscular walls stretch and, as they do so, send messages to the appetite center or "appestat" in the brain. But these are not instant. It is thought that it takes about 20 minutes from the start of a meal for the appestat to register that you are full up. So chewing well and eating slowly – for instance by putting your knife and fork down between mouthfuls – can be a good way of feeling full on less food and, ultimately, losing weight.

DON'T SCRATCH AN ITCH

There is nothing more irritating than an itch, but this adage is pure common sense because, in the end, scratching will only prolong the agony.

Long-used herbal preparations for soothing itchy skin include lavender ointment and an infusion of dried marigold flowers.

It is histamine that makes you want to scratch an itch. This is the chemical released into the skin when you are bitten by an insect or stung by a nettle or jellyfish, or when you have a disease like chickenpox. It is also produced when you develop an allergic reaction to something that touches your skin, like soap or the metal nickel, or to a certain food. What happens when you scratch is that even more histamine is produced, making you want to scratch even more.

Over-the-counter antihistamines will help the symptoms, but it is well worth tracking down the cause of an allergy so as to avoid it in future. Granny's remedies for itching were calamine lotion, a diluted (1 in 40) solution of carbolic acid, or a warm soda bath before bed. For young children tempted to scratch the treatment was severe: "[They] should be prevented from scratching by sewing the sleeves of their nightdress to the body of the garment, or by loosely tying the hands to the waist."

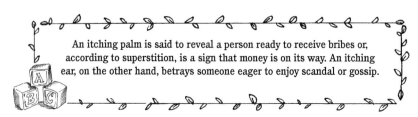

An itching palm is said to reveal a person ready to receive bribes or, according to superstition, is a sign that money is on its way. An itching ear, on the other hand, betrays someone eager to enjoy scandal or gossip.

BRUSH YOUR HAIR A HUNDRED TIMES AT NIGHT

A hundred is too many, but brushing certainly makes
hair shine by stimulating the oil glands in the scalp,
and distributing oil evenly along the length of the
tresses. But overbrushing can damage both
hair and scalp.

The other problem with brushes and combs is that they can pull out
hairs or make the ends split or break off. Too much brushing may
overstimulate the oil glands and
make the hair too greasy, especially
in the teenage years when the
production of sebum, the natural,
protective hair oil, is being boosted
by a surge of hormones.

*A lock of hair was a lovers'
keepsake and a sign of fidelity.
Locks of hair were often exchanged
before men went off to war.*

It would have taken a great deal of brushing or combing before bedtime
to untangle some of the complex women's hairstyles of the past, and even
a girl's plaits if her hair was naturally curly. In the days when long hair
was *de rigueur*, standard nighttime advice lectured against the use of fine
combs, which would "tear out hair unnecessarily," and recommended that
to protect it from strain on the roots during sleep "hair should never be
fastened up very tightly...the more loosely it is plaited the better."

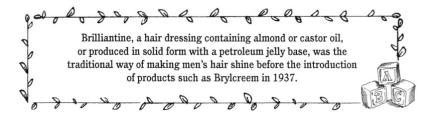

Brilliantine, a hair dressing containing almond or castor oil,
or produced in solid form with a petroleum jelly base, was the
traditional way of making men's hair shine before the introduction
of products such as Brylcreem in 1937.

CHOOSE PINK FOR A GIRL, BLUE FOR A BOY

When it comes to good fortune in colors, girls get the raw deal. Because, in a family, boys were once more highly prized than girls, they became linked with the color that is traditionally associated with good fortune.

The all-in-one stretch "Babygro" was devised by a father frustrated with dressing his child. It was patented in 1959.

Blue, the color of the sky, has long been a lucky hue, and the *Book of Numbers*, written in the 5th century, advised the children of Israel to protect themselves by wearing garments fringed with "a ribband of blue." Wearing a blue ribbon or necklace was also thought to protect against illness – but so too was donning a red one. A red thread worn around the neck was supposed, from the 1st century AD onwards, to guard against problems as diverse as lunacy and a witch's evil eye.

Swaddling bands were the usual clothing for babies until the 1700s. After this a layette including gowns and petticoats was gradually introduced. Only in the early 1900s did boys and girls come to be dressed differently, and it was the 1930s before the fashion for pink and blue really took hold.

A MATTER OF LUCK
- A bride invokes blue's lucky powers when she chooses "something blue" to wear along with something old, something new and something borrowed.
- It is said that, for luck, newborn babies should be dressed by pulling the clothes over their feet, not their heads.
- In Ireland until the 20th century, boy babies were often dressed as girls in an attempt to deceive the "boy-seeking Devil."

DON'T SWALLOW CHERRY STONES – THEY CAN GIVE YOU APPENDICITIS

Lack of fiber in the diet, not pips and stones, is thought to be the most likely cause of appendicitis. Fruit stones will, very rarely, lodge there, but are most likely to pass through the digestive system and be ejected from the body intact.

Appendicitis – infection, obstruction and inflammation of the "redundant" 3½ inches (9 cm) pouch in the large intestine – is most common in young people between the ages of 8 and 25. Usually, there is no obvious reason for the problem, but it does seem to be associated with constipation, and the "stones" sometimes detected in an appendix during surgery are in fact small, hard feces.

The typical symptoms of appendicitis are a pain around the navel, which (though not always in children) moves downwards and to the

The cherry stones on your plate were counted in the old rhyme "Tinker, tailor, soldier, sailor, rich man, poor man, beggar man, thief," to predict who you would marry.

right, and is worse after the release of pressure if the area is pressed. Acute appendicitis needs emergency surgery; if the problem organ ruptures it can lead to potentially fatal septicemia (blood poisoning).

The term "appendicitis" was first used in America by Dr. Reginald Fitz in 1886. In Britain, the first appendectomy was performed on Samuel Smith at the London Hospital in 1888 by the Dorset surgeon Frederick Treves. But while Fitz believed in surgery immediately following diagnosis, Treves recommended waiting five days; the belief cost him the life of his own daughter, who died from a ruptured appendix.

Some experts still believe in the "grumbling" appendix – painful attacks that resolve themselves spontaneously – but others think that an appendix either "roars" because it is inflamed or is healthy and silent.

ALWAYS SLEEP WITH THE BEDROOM WINDOW OPEN

Good ventilation in the bedroom, to keep up the oxygen levels and to ensure that the air does not become stale and smelly, was a must long before our homes were centrally heated and air conditioned, and is still advisable except in cold weather.

In the 1930s home, bedroom ventilation was provided by the Boyle air inlet – an opening in the wall with a flap inserted that could be opened or closed as desired.

When rooms were heated with coal fires, and sanitation was often basic at best, keeping smells out of the bedroom – and indeed from the whole house – was as important as letting in fresh air to benefit the lungs. In the 19th and early 20th centuries, parents were especially aware of the dangers of "sewer gas," which might be emanating from drains clogged with rotting wastes, and carbon dioxide (which they called carbonic acid gas) produced by gas and oil lamps.

In modern, well-insulated homes, one of the greatest problems arising from keeping bedroom (or any other) windows closed is the accumulation of moisture in the air, which encourages condensation and mold growth. As well as looking unsightly, many of these can provoke allergies in susceptible people. Lack of ventilation also leads to the build-up of pollutants – produced by anything from room fresheners to glues – which can inflict a home, as well as an office, with "sick building syndrome."

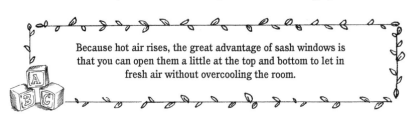

Because hot air rises, the great advantage of sash windows is that you can open them a little at the top and bottom to let in fresh air without overcooling the room.

DON'T SWIM UNTIL AT LEAST AN HOUR AFTER A MEAL

The logic here is that immediately after eating the legs may be more susceptible to cramp, increasing the risk of drowning. And although modern medicine takes a somewhat less prescriptive view, it remains wise to be cautious of heavy meals and remote beaches.

It is a fact that immediately after a meal, blood is diverted to the stomach and digestive system. As a result it is drawn away from the arms and legs, depriving their muscles of water, nutrients and the minerals they need to contract smoothly and painlessly. Equally, there is a known link between

In 1927 the Girl Guides' Manual *declared British girls to be well behind their contemporaries in Norway and Sweden, of little "real use" until they could swim, and that "to learn swimming is no more difficult than to learn bicycling."*

regular, persistent cramp – strong localized muscle contractions – and poor circulation. The counter argument to this is that once you start exercising, blood begins to flow freely through the limbs, slowing down the digestive process and promoting movement.

If cramp does strike while you're swimming, you need to get back on land as quickly as possible and stretch the affected limb, or get someone to do it for you. Try to float on your back, breathe in deeply, and paddle with your arms both for buoyancy and to maneuver yourself to safety.

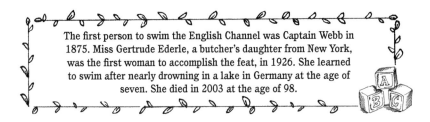

The first person to swim the English Channel was Captain Webb in 1875. Miss Gertrude Ederle, a butcher's daughter from New York, was the first woman to accomplish the feat, in 1926. She learned to swim after nearly drowning in a lake in Germany at the age of seven. She died in 2003 at the age of 98.

EAT YOUR GREENS

• •

Unfortunately for reluctant children, and some adults too, greens really do you good. So do vegetables in any other color. Eat them and you have a good chance of keeping healthy into old age.

The substances in vegetables that pack the most powerful punch are the antioxidants, which include vitamin C, lycopene, contained in red fruits like tomatoes, and beta-carotene, the substance that makes carrots and sweet potatoes orange. In their normal day-to-day metabolism, cells release free radicals, including unstable oxygen molecules, which antioxidants mop up. Left unchecked, free radicals can damage body cells (a possible precursor of cancer) and contribute in the build-up of the fatty deposits in the arteries that can cause heart disease and strokes.

There's more. Vegetables contain fiber to help keep you regular. Beans and peas are especially useful as they contain soluble, easily absorbed fiber. Fresh or frozen, they can help the health of everything from your eyesight to your immune system.

But maybe you can't help disliking green vegetables. Some 20–25 percent of us are "supertasters," with taste buds genetically programmed to be so sensitive to the bitter chemicals in vegetables (especially brassicas) that they simply can't tolerate them. However, these nasty tasting substances are believed to have anti-cancer properties.

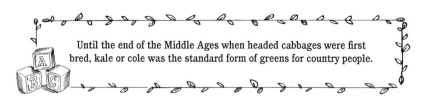

Until the end of the Middle Ages when headed cabbages were first bred, kale or cole was the standard form of greens for country people.

DON'T GO SWIMMING IF YOU HAVE A VERRUCA

It's not swimming that is the problem but the fact that verrucae – warts on the soles of the feet – are highly infectious. Walking barefoot around a changing room effectively spreads the problem to others.

Verrucae, known medically as plantar warts, are caused by the human papilloma virus. The best treatment is the application of a wart-dissolving liquid, which can be bought over the counter, but persistent verrucae may need cryosurgery: freezing off with liquid nitrogen. Before this neat and almost painless treatment, children with verrucae or warts would have them surgically removed under a local anesthetic. Bleeding could be profuse and the post-operative pain excruciating.

To portray someone "warts and all" is to give the whole picture. When the 17th-century artist Peter Lely was painting the portrait of Oliver Cromwell the sitter is reported to have said, "Remark all these roughnesses, pimples, warts, and everything as you see me."

WARTS AND ALL
Warts are notoriously hard to shift, which may explain why there are so many traditional treatments, such as:

- Sap from the greater celandine.
- Strong vinegar (acetic acid).
- Hypnosis.
- Rubbing with meat, then secretly burying the meat.
- Selling the wart to someone.
- Passing a wart to a dead person in a funeral cortege.

WASH YOUR HANDS BEFORE MEALS

The simple reason is that it is possible to ingest food poisoning bacteria with your food, particularly if you eat with your fingers. Even more vital is to wash after going to the lavatory, where potentially deadly bacteria can get on to the hands with ease.

Washing with ordinary soap is still the best way of killing harmful bacteria – and, as a bonus, viruses such as those that transmit colds and flu – but it is worth taking the trouble to open your fingers wide and rub both hands together to get the job done thoroughly. Regular nail brushing is helpful, too.

Staphylococcus aureus, *Escherichia (E.) coli* and species of *Salmonella* are the food poisoning bacteria particularly worth killing. They make us ill by releasing toxins that inflame the lining of the intestine, causing vomiting and diarrhea and, unless counteracted by the intake of plenty of fluids, harmful dehydration. As well as keeping your hands clean remember to keep hot food hot (140–165°F/60–70°C) and cold food

There are some evil stains that even the strongest soap will not remove. "Will these hands ne'er be clean?" moaned the murderous Lady Macbeth in Shakespeare's play.

cold (34–40°F/1–4°C). Store meat and fish away from other foods in the refrigerator and don't eat decaying or suspect food – throw it out.

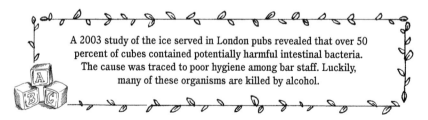

A 2003 study of the ice served in London pubs revealed that over 50 percent of cubes contained potentially harmful intestinal bacteria. The cause was traced to poor hygiene among bar staff. Luckily, many of these organisms are killed by alcohol.

TO CURE HICCUPS DRINK "BACKWARDS" FROM A GLASS OF WATER

Best done over a bowl to save spills, this is as well worth trying as other remedies. These include sipping through a straw, holding your breath, eating a teaspoon of sugar or chanting the Scottish rhyme "Hiccup, hiccup, gang [go] away, Come again another day; Hiccup, hiccup when I bake, I'll give to you a butter cake."

Hiccups happen when the diaphragm, the tough sheet of muscle that separates the abdomen from the chest, goes into spasm. It is the smooth, regular, up-and-down movement of the diaphragm that naturally allows the lungs room to expand with air as you take in each breath, but swallowing air as you laugh, eating too fast, or sipping the cold bubbles of carbon dioxide in a fizzy drink can all set off an attack of the hiccups.

MORE HICCUP CURES
Try breaking the rhythm of the spasms with any of these other well-tried remedies:

- Suck an ice cube.
- Sniff some pepper and make yourself sneeze (the old-fashioned way was with snuff).
- Drink a mouthful of cold water.
- Sip a teaspoon of whisky.
- Take a teaspoon of lemon juice with a pinch of salt added.
- Get someone to drop a cold spoon or key down your back, inside your clothes.
- Make three "marks of Christ," first on your tongue, then on your head and third on your chest.

Hiccups are often associated with eating certain foods and with heartburn, which if persistent needs a doctor's attention and treatment. If you get hiccups, heartburn or both, try eating smaller, more frequent meals and avoiding spices and acid-provokers such as onions, garlic, caffeine, mint and cigarette smoke.

The world record for the longest continuous bout of hiccups is held by Charles Osborne from Anthon, Iowa. His hiccups started in 1922 at a rate of 40 times per minute, slowed to 20, and eventually stopped in February 1990 – a total of 68 years.

SUGAR ROTS YOUR TEETH

Not directly, but sugar is the favorite food of the bacterium *Streptococcus mutans*, which as it feeds, leaks into your mouth an acid powerful enough to dissolve tooth enamel, the hardest substance in the body. Worst of all are the acids found in fizzy drinks, even low sugar (diet) ones.

A tooth decays when the enamel is eroded and bacteria get inside, breaking down the hard, calcium-rich substance of which it is made. Left untreated, the pulp of an affected tooth, which contains blood vessels and nerves, may be attacked, and the tooth can die a painful death. And the bad news is that drinking four or more glasses of fizzy drinks a day raises the chances of enamel erosion by over 250 percent because of the action of the phosphoric acid they contain.

The good news is that even if you have a sweet tooth there are lots of things you can do to neutralize the acid in your mouth. Start by making more saliva – the naturally alkaline

When sugar first reached Europe in around AD 800 it was considered so valuable that it was used as a medicine, not a food. In medieval times sugar was routinely given to sickly children to improve their health.

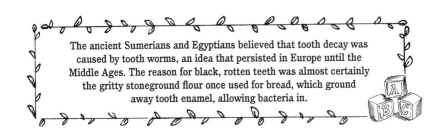

The ancient Sumerians and Egyptians believed that tooth decay was caused by tooth worms, an idea that persisted in Europe until the Middle Ages. The reason for black, rotten teeth was almost certainly the gritty stoneground flour once used for bread, which ground away tooth enamel, allowing bacteria in.

substance that flows into the mouth to help digestion – by chewing sugarless gum for 20 minutes after a meal. Eating a small piece of cheese or drinking a glass of milk can have the same effect.

Herbal mouthwashes made from soaking dried marigold heads or thyme leaves in boiling water are age-old ways of keeping tooth decay at bay. Brushing is essential, and a more recent addition to the anti-decay armory is fluoride toothpaste, first sold by Procter and Gamble in 1955 with the brand name "Crest." Fluoride strengthens tooth enamel and makes it more resistant to decay.

EAT BREAD AND BUTTER BEFORE CAKE

The golden rule of the nursery was an admonition against greed at the tea table, especially for children. Equally, for frugal parents, it was a way of ensuring that hungry offspring satiated their appetites with inexpensive bread and viewed cakes as a treat.

Tea was originally a meal served before bed because, until the 19th century, dinner was eaten at midday, supper in the early evening and tea was the last meal of the day. As more men began to work outside the home, supper became later and later, and eventually tea was a meal that filled the afternoon gap between luncheon and dinner, or sustained children after their school work was completed and office workers when they arrived home.

The "polite" middle class tea consisted of small sandwiches and cakes, but for working class families it contained eggs, meat or both. As well as eating their bread or toast first, well-mannered children, when it was time for cake, would be expected to "take the first that comes" rather than reaching across a serving plate for the delicacy they fancied most.

Taking tea also became popular in the USA in the 19th century, with five o'clock the most popular hour. The housewife was advised not to omit "the porcelain platters bearing wafer-like slices of buttered bread, cakelets, and, if you would be thoroughly English, a shape of hot buttered bread…"

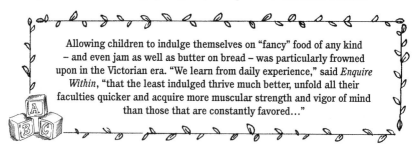

Allowing children to indulge themselves on "fancy" food of any kind – and even jam as well as butter on bread – was particularly frowned upon in the Victorian era. "We learn from daily experience," said *Enquire Within*, "that the least indulged thrive much better, unfold all their faculties quicker and acquire more muscular strength and vigor of mind than those that are constantly favored…"

CHEESE GIVES YOU NIGHTMARES

Not just a piece of everyday health guidance on late evening eating, but a link with ancient medical practice and legends linking cheese with witchcraft.

To avoid nightmares, the accepted advice is that any food that is hard to digest should be shunned at bedtime. This was the belief of the Greek physician Galen. Those prone to nightmares should also, it was said, take their last meal at least three hours before sleeping and avoid doing mental work for the same period.

According to modern science, the problems with cheese stem from the chemical tyramine, which is made by bacteria in cheese. Tyramine not only raises the blood pressure – a stress symptom associated with nightmares – but can, in susceptible people, alter the activity of nerves in the brain and bring on migraines.

Children's nightmares usually begin when, at about the age of three, their imaginations start to develop and expand. And while much of the old advice still holds good – never speak impatiently to a child who wakes in fear; leave a light on for a child who dreads the dark; avoid overstimulation and creepy stories at night; talk through and "exorcise" the dream – parents today, unlike their counterparts of a century ago, are unlikely to think of constipation or "faulty feeding" as nightmares' primary cause.

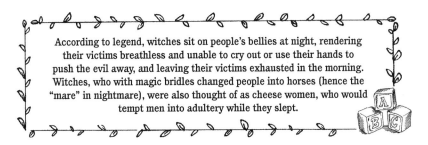

According to legend, witches sit on people's bellies at night, rendering their victims breathless and unable to cry out or use their hands to push the evil away, and leaving their victims exhausted in the morning. Witches, who with magic bridles changed people into horses (hence the "mare" in nightmare), were also thought of as cheese women, who would tempt men into adultery while they slept.

DON'T EAT OFF YOUR KNIFE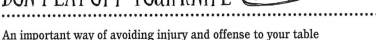

An important way of avoiding injury and offense to your table companions, this is also one of many rules of good table manners set down since the paired use of knife and fork.

The custom nowadays is to cut with your knife and eat from your fork. At a formal meal, separate knives and forks are provided for each course, plus an extra knife for spreading butter on bread. The knives are placed with their sharp blades facing inwards in the order in which they need to be

Round-tipped table knives were introduced in the 17th century after the French statesman Cardinal Richelieu declared himself disgusted by seeing his eating companions picking their teeth with the pointed tips of their knives.

used, starting from the outside. At a banquet you might still be expected to use a knife and fork to cut and peel fresh fruit served as part of dessert, in which case a sharp fruit knife will be provided.

Children need practice to use knives and forks properly. Emily Post's *Blue Book* of 1922 issues the stern warning that "Food and table implements are not playthings, nor is the dining room table a playground" and warns against allowing children to "construct a tent out of two forks, or an automobile chassis out of tumblers and knives…" "Don't play with your food" is still a frequent admonishment.

KNIFE LORE

Knives, being valuable possessions, are the subjects of many customs and superstitions:

- Don't give a knife as a gift: it will sever love or friendship. To prevent this, the recipient should offer a penny payment in return.
- A knife that falls from the table signals the imminent arrival of an unexpected guest.
- In a thunderstorm put the knives away, they will attract lightning.
- Knives that are crossed mean a quarrel, bad luck or a death in the family.
- If you toast bread on a knife you'll be poor all your life.

DON'T EAT BETWEEN MEALS

• •

When mealtimes were strictly kept, and children pressured to clear their plates, eating between meals was frowned on because it was deemed to dull the appetite. And in many weight-control regimes, snacking is regarded as a sure way of breaking the diet.

The truth is, whether eating between meals is healthy or not all depends on what you eat, how much and in what context. Stuffing yourself with high fat, high salt, high carbohydrate snacks can be a sure way of piling on the weight, like one 33-stone (210 kg) 6 ft 6 in (1.95 m) 17-year-old who confessed to snacking daily on sweets, biscuits, cakes and chips between meals and late at night.

By contrast, if you are on a low-calorie diet, eating two small

In Britain, schools were permitted by the 1926 Education (Provision of Meals) Act to provide free or low-cost meals for schoolchildren and a daily bottle of milk. This measure alone helped to reduce child mortality rates considerably.

100-calorie snacks a day between main meals not only helps to stave off hunger pangs but assists in keeping your blood sugar levels constant. This puts less strain on your pancreas, the organ that secretes the hormone insulin vital to sugar metabolism.

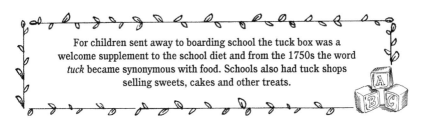

For children sent away to boarding school the tuck box was a welcome supplement to the school diet and from the 1750s the word *tuck* became synonymous with food. Schools also had tuck shops selling sweets, cakes and other treats.

KEEP YOUR ELBOWS OFF THE TABLE

Or, as grandmother used to warn, "all joints on the table will be carved." Yet another of the old rules once sternly enforced on children, to their dread. Particularly undesirable, say the etiquette police, is to sit with the left elbow on the table while eating with the right hand, or while lifting a glass.

For leaning forward in animated after-dinner conversation, it is said, resting on the elbows is perfectly permissible. But "Miss Manners" in her *Ultimate Handbook on Modern Etiquette* maintains that: "Elbows are banned during eating because of the awkward, cranelike motion it gives to the hand on the other end of the elbow... Also it is a delightfully easy error to catch children in, whose other errors may be more subtle."

An itching elbow is said to be a sign that you will encounter a new or strange bedfellow.

The elbow – the joint that, together with the shoulder, gives the arm its mobility, and when bent allows us distance from our neighbor – is actually composed of two joints. The major joint is the hinge where the two forearm bones, the radius and the ulna, meet the humerus, the bone of the upper arm. At the second, the superior radio-ulnar joint, the top of the radius articulates with a notch in the adjacent ulna, allowing the arm to pivot.

DON'T SQUEEZE SPOTS, THEY'LL TURN SEPTIC

Squeezing spots is an easy way of introducing bacteria that can exacerbate the problem, delay healing and even leave scars. But it is a myth that full-blown acne can be caused by spot squeezing, lack of washing or eating chocolate.

Spots erupt when sebum, the skin's oily secretion, blocks the pores. As a result, blackheads form and bacteria may proliferate, causing pus-filled pimples. These are the scourge of adolescence because this is the time when, under hormonal influence, the sebaceous glands generate additional sebum production. In severe acne, the

Many diseases, such as chickenpox, erupt in characteristic types of spots. Pock and pox are old words for spots, particularly associated with the deadly smallpox.

blocked pores may develop into hard cysts that, when they eventually disappear, leave pits in the skin. True acne needs medical attention – for both physical and psychological reasons – but home treatment to rid the skin of excess oil can help the teenager who gets the occasional spot.

Tea tree oil is a long-used aboriginal treatment for spots. Great burdock is an old English country remedy, and recent experiments have shown that burdock root (available from herbalists in capsule form) contains substances that help to kill both bacteria and fungi.

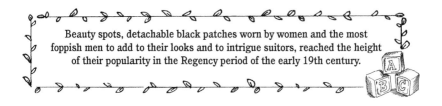

Beauty spots, detachable black patches worn by women and the most foppish men to add to their looks and to intrigue suitors, reached the height of their popularity in the Regency period of the early 19th century.

COUNT SHEEP TO FALL ASLEEP

The age-old remedy for getting to sleep is only one of many strategies for nodding off. It is the rhythm and monotony of sheep-counting that is believed to help the brain change its electrical rhythms from the pattern typical of wakefulness into that of sleep.

If this doesn't work, there are lots of other angles to try, like "taking a walk" around a favorite place or telling yourself a bedtime story. The trick is to help the brain to turn off its customary "noise" so that you forget your everyday worries and fall asleep. If all that fails, then get up and do something useful.

Herbs of all kinds have long been used in remedies for insomnia, including a pillow filled with hops, lavender or valerian root. A traditional "slumber tea" for children was made from an infusion of valerian root, dried lemon balm, chamomile leaves, bitter orange blossom and rosehips, sweetened with honey.

NO REST
The causes of unwanted wakefulness are many and varied:

- Cold feet.
- Bad ventilation of the bedroom.
- Uncomfortable bed, unsuitable bedclothes.
- A hot room.
- Hunger or a full stomach.
- Too high or too low a pillow.
- Noise.
- Too much light in the room.
- Tea or coffee taken late in the evening.
- Mental or physical overwork and exhaustion.
- Want of exercise.
- Worry, financial anxiety, domestic troubles.
- Retiring at irregular hours.

BREAST IS BEST

Not just because breast milk is the natural food for babies but also because it imparts some immunity against disease. What's more, it is believed to lower the risks of high blood pressure, heart disease and strokes in later life.

The fluid that flows from a new mother's breasts in the first 72 hours after giving birth is colostrum, which is rich in infection-fighting antibodies that prevent intestinal infections. It also contains a substance that produces an insulin-like growth factor, which helps to stimulate muscle growth.

The nutritious sugars in breast milk (oligosaccharides) are also thought to kill harmful bacteria – notably food poisoning

Babies have been fed from cups and bottles from ancient times, containers being made from materials as diverse as cows' horns, terracotta, leather and pewter.

bacteria such as *E. coli* – and to promote the proliferation of "friendly" bacteria in the gut, which may boost the immune system and improve babies' resistance to allergies. The substances that help maintain a healthy blood pressure in adults who were breast-fed as babies are long-chain polyunsaturated fatty acids, components of the fats in human milk.

Before the arrival of "formula," a wet nurse was the only solution for women unable to breast-feed, and for orphans, although the upper classes employed wet nurses for social reasons – Queen Victoria decried breast-feeding as "making a cow of oneself." Wet nurses were chosen with care; brunettes were preferred to blondes or redheads because their milk was considered to be more nutritious and their temperaments more "balanced."

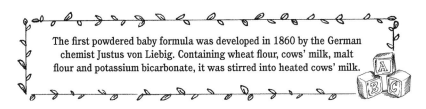

The first powdered baby formula was developed in 1860 by the German chemist Justus von Liebig. Containing wheat flour, cows' milk, malt flour and potassium bicarbonate, it was stirred into heated cows' milk.

177

EAT SPINACH FOR IRON

•••

Advice born of human error. Spinach is not the best vegetable source of this essential mineral – watercress and broccoli have more, and meat and oily fish are best of all – but it is good for you in other ways.

It was a slip of the pen, perpetrated in the 1890s, which gave spinach its unwarranted reputation. When calculating the vegetable's iron content, a food analyst put the decimal point in the wrong position, implying that spinach contained ten times more iron than it actually did. Nearly a century later, in 1981, the mistake was finally rectified, but not until after millions of children had been pressed to eat spinach against their wishes.

Popeye the Sailor Man, quantity consumer of spinach and possessed, as a result, of bulging muscles, was a cartoon character created in the 1930s by EC "Elzie" Segar. A Popeye statue stands today in Segar's hometown of Chester, Illinois.

The body needs iron to help build red blood cells, and particularly hemoglobin, which carries life-giving oxygen around the system. Without enough iron anemia sets in, typified by lack of stamina and breathlessness, but not necessarily accompanied by the pale inner eyelids that tradition suggests.

Iron in food comes in two kinds. Meat and oily fish contain heme iron, which is chemically partway to blood corpuscle configuration. The iron in vegetables and fruit – including apricots, lentils and nuts – is the non-heme variety. This needs vitamin C to assist its absorption from the digestive system. Conversely, the caffeine in tea and coffee can actually prevent non-heme iron from being absorbed.

Spinach scores highly for folate, also essential to blood formation and first identified when extracted from spinach in the 1940s. Folate helps the efficient healing of cuts and wounds, heart health and, during the first three months of pregnancy, reduces the risk of spina bifida.

EAT PRUNES TO KEEP YOU REGULAR

Prunes do the trick, but you should be wary of eating these dried plums in quantity as they can cause nasty flatulence.

Compared with other fruits prunes give constipation the double whammy. They not only contain fiber, which when fermented in the bowel increases in bulk, pushing food residues down the gut, but also isatin, a chemical that stimulates the muscles of the bowel.

The daily bowel movement was long considered a mark of good health but doctors today are more worried by a change in a person's natural rhythm than in the rhythm itself. Under the strict regimes that persisted

The savory devils on horseback is made from prunes wrapped in thin slices of bacon and fried.

from the 19th to the mid 20th century, children would be questioned about their daily "performance" and might be confined in the lavatory for hours or dosed with the bitter herb cascara.

Prunes were once regularly served for school lunch. Nigel Molesworth, hero of Geoffrey Willans and Ronald Searle's 1953 best seller *Down With Skool!* (and famous for his intuitive spelling) recounts his nightmare "The Revolt of the Prunes" in which a "tribe of savvage prunes who lived in a blak mass in the skool pantry" leap from their plates, take the boys prisoner and attack the headmaster.

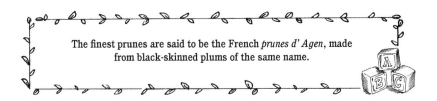

The finest prunes are said to be the French *prunes d' Agen*, made from black-skinned plums of the same name.

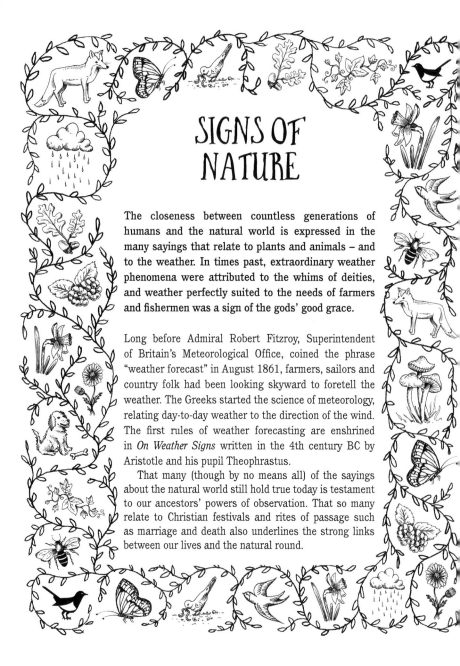

SIGNS OF NATURE

The closeness between countless generations of humans and the natural world is expressed in the many sayings that relate to plants and animals – and to the weather. In times past, extraordinary weather phenomena were attributed to the whims of deities, and weather perfectly suited to the needs of farmers and fishermen was a sign of the gods' good grace.

Long before Admiral Robert Fitzroy, Superintendent of Britain's Meteorological Office, coined the phrase "weather forecast" in August 1861, farmers, sailors and country folk had been looking skyward to foretell the weather. The Greeks started the science of meteorology, relating day-to-day weather to the direction of the wind. The first rules of weather forecasting are enshrined in *On Weather Signs* written in the 4th century BC by Aristotle and his pupil Theophrastus.

That many (though by no means all) of the sayings about the natural world still hold true today is testament to our ancestors' powers of observation. That so many relate to Christian festivals and rites of passage such as marriage and death also underlines the strong links between our lives and the natural round.

RING ROUND THE MOON, SNOW SOON

In winter, it may quite possibly be so. Or the ring could be a sign that rain is on the way, depending on how cold it is.

On a winter's night a pale ring or halo around the moon – shimmering with faint rainbow colors, with the red on the inside – is a magnificent sight, often more spectacular because many of the stars are blotted out by cloud. Sometimes it lasts for only a few minutes, but if it persists for longer you may see the different colors strengthen and fade as the ice crystals move about, turning and swirling in the cloud.

Comprising the moon's halo are millions of minute, hexagonal ice crystals, often borne on moisture-

Halos form around the sun in exactly the same way as those around the moon, but it is dangerous to look at them directly. They, too, are good predictors of rain.

laden cirrostratus cloud. In its infancy, this cloud is thin and high enough – about 22,000 feet (6,000 m) above the ground – to be penetrated by the sun's rays illuminating the moon from below the horizon. We see a halo because each of the ice crystals bends the sun's light twice. If the cloud then thickens and lowers, snow or rain will almost certainly fall. If the cloud disperses then it won't.

Just to confuse, there is another phenomenon, the corona, which invariably includes a brownish ring, with bluish-white colors towards the inside. If red is there at all it will be to the outside, not the inside. However this does not constitute a weather prediction.

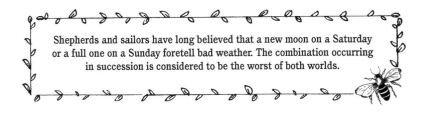

Shepherds and sailors have long believed that a new moon on a Saturday or a full one on a Sunday foretell bad weather. The combination occurring in succession is considered to be the worst of both worlds.

WHEN SWALLOWS FLY LOW, RAIN IS ON THE WAY

• •

Although swallows rarely fly very high in the sky, these graceful birds have been used as weather predictors since ancient times.

The Roman poet Virgil was one of the earliest recorders of typical swallow behavior:

Wet weather seldom hurts the most unwise;
So plain the signs, such prophets are the skies'
The swallow skims the river's watery face;
The frogs renew the croaks of their loquacious race.

On a fine day, as they hunt for flying insects, which they scoop up into their wide, deep bills, swallows will alternately glide high in the air to catch groups of weak prey, drawn up from the ground by warm air currents, and swoop down lower over open ground or water where large insects abound. But when the air pressure falls and the air is full of moisture (whether or not it is going to rain) insects descend much closer to the ground, and therefore so do the swallows that pursue them.

When it's wet and windy, insects go to ground or stay lodged in vegetation or in the lee of a hedge or wall. Then the swallows have to travel farther from their nests – to places such as rivers or sewage farms – and will sometimes pick insects off tree leaves or even forage for food on the ground. Near the coast swallows will feed low on sandhoppers and flies.

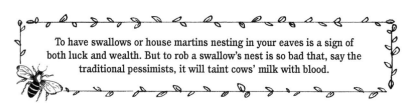

To have swallows or house martins nesting in your eaves is a sign of both luck and wealth. But to rob a swallow's nest is so bad that, say the traditional pessimists, it will taint cows' milk with blood.

WHEN GORSE IS OUT OF BLOOM, KISSING'S OUT OF FASHION

This English country saying acknowledges the fact that gorse can be seen in flower throughout the year – it may also refer to the prevalence of gorse in lovers' traditional meeting places.

The botanical key to this saying is that, in England and Wales, different species of gorse – all with bright yellow pea-like flowers and a wonderfully heady scent – grow close together. In a mild year the common gorse (*Ulex europaeus*) flowers from late winter to mid summer. After it has finished blooming, two rarer species come into flower for the rest of the year: the western gorse (*U. gallii*), which grows on acid, western moors, and in the south and east of England, the dwarf or lesser gorse (*U. minor*).

It is said that Carolus Linnaeus, the Swedish botanist who devised the system of plant classification, fell to his knees in wonder when he first saw gorse in bloom. The location was probably Putney Heath, near London; the year, 1736. Through history, gorse has had many domestic uses, from fuel to cattle fodder, and for sweeping.

KISSING FACTS
- The American confectioner Hershey has been selling chocolate "kisses" since 1902.
- A gambler will kiss the dice for good luck before a throw.
- A kiss conveys the winner's joy on receiving a coveted trophy.
- A kiss on the fingers, accompanied by an extravagant hand gesture, says "goodbye."

ANIMALS CAN PREDICT EARTHQUAKES

Earthquakes strike with a suddenness unpredictable to human senses, but some observers are convinced that animals change their behavior before disaster strikes.

A few days before the earthquake that shook Haicheng in China in 1975, cows, horses and other mammals began to get restless. Chickens were reluctant to return to their roosts, birds took flight and there were reports of "dazed" rats and snakes that seemed to be frozen to the ground. An evacuation was ordered and many lives saved. Ahead of the disastrous tsunami in December 2004, animals including elephants and monkeys were observed moving to high ground.

Many animals have senses well beyond the range of humans. Insects can see ultraviolet light, bats detect ultrasound and some fish can sense electric fields.

Animals, it seems, are able to sense and respond to the small tremors of foreshocks that occur before the cataclysm. To accomplish this they are probably using their organs of hearing and balance (combined in the ear in mammals). They may also be responding, with their organs of smell, to the presence of gases such as methane released from below the earth's surface just prior to an earthquake.

What makes animals less reliable predictors is that in many earthquakes there are no foreshocks. Equally, seismologists know where earthquakes are likely to occur – at the "faults" between the earth's tectonic plates, which constantly slide past each other – but not when.

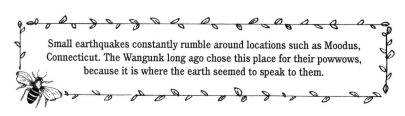

Small earthquakes constantly rumble around locations such as Moodus, Connecticut. The Wangunk long ago chose this place for their powwows, because it is where the earth seemed to speak to them.

CATS WILL ALWAYS FIND THEIR WAY HOME

There is plenty of proof that this is true, and some cats have journeys of thousands of miles on record. But it is an old wives' tale that putting butter on a cat's paws will stop it wandering away after a house move.

In 1981, records *The Guinness Book of Oddities*, a Turk named Mehmet Tunc was on a journey from Germany with his cat Minosch. At the Turkish border the cat disappeared, only to turn up 61 days later 1,500 miles (2,400 km) away at the Tunc family home. Another cat, named Sugar, who was hampered by a deformed hip, even crossed the Rockies, at the rate of 100 miles (160 km) a month, to be reunited with her owners who had moved from Anderson, California, to Gage, Oklahoma. And in 2011, after her family moved house, a tabby named Jessie traveled over 2,000 miles (3,200 km) across Australia to her previous home.

Cats find their way, it is thought, by using the sun as both a compass and a clock. Like migratory birds they may also be able to detect subtle changes in the earth's magnetic field. Nearer to home, they use their sense of smell, which, as in humans, has a strong link to the memory.

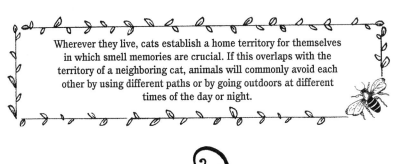

Wherever they live, cats establish a home territory for themselves in which smell memories are crucial. If this overlaps with the territory of a neighboring cat, animals will commonly avoid each other by using different paths or by going outdoors at different times of the day or night.

DOGS CAN SMELL STRANGERS

Except for identical twins who, because our personal odors are inherited, share exactly the same smell, molecule for molecule, dogs can easily detect the difference between individuals. The record breakers are bloodhounds, which have been known to follow trails several days old, or stretching 100 miles (160 km) and more.

Dogs have a sense of smell vastly superior to that of humans. This has much to do with the size and composition of their olfactory epithelium, the sheet of tissue at the top of the nasal cavity that is sensitive to aromas. This is 20 times bigger in dogs than it is in humans and is supplied with more than a hundred times as many smell-sensitive cells.

Dogs are particularly good at detecting the substances that comprise human sweat, notably butyric acid, and it is this that makes them so good at finding the buried victims of avalanches and earthquakes. This is proved in the pebble test. Six people pick up a pebble and throw it as far as they can. The dog then sniffs the hand of one person and will successfully retrieve the pebble thrown by them.

In the wild, dogs use smell as a vital means of finding food located a long way off, for enhancing the strength of the pack and for finding a mate. The reason why dogs occasionally roll in cow or horse dung may be to disguise their smell from rabbits and other potential live food. It may also be a signal for members of the pack to gather round before a hunt.

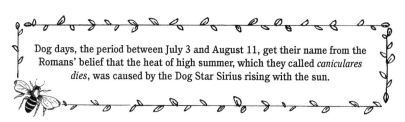

Dog days, the period between July 3 and August 11, get their name from the Romans' belief that the heat of high summer, which they called *caniculares dies*, was caused by the Dog Star Sirius rising with the sun.

COWS LIE DOWN WHEN IT'S GOING TO RAIN

They do – and they don't! In other words they are poor weather forecasters, although some farmers claim that cows predict storms by exhibiting bad-tempered behavior. Cows with any sense will take shelter from a downpour by standing or lying down under nearby trees.

The truth about cow behavior is that, rain or shine, they generally stand up to eat in the morning and evening, and lie down for anything up to 12 hours to chew the cud during the rest of the day or night. Being herd animals, what one does, all (or most) do, so when you pass a field of cows you are very likely to see them all eating or all chewing.

According to country lore, if a cow trespasses into your garden, expect a death in the family.

Cattle chew the cud to get maximum benefit from hard-to-digest grass. A cow's stomach has four compartments, which are used in a specific order. Ingested grass enters the large first stomach, where it is softened and overflows into the smaller second stomach. From both first and second stomachs food is regurgitated in small portions and ruminated. It is then swallowed into the third stomach and finally into the fourth or "true" stomach.

ANIMAL RAIN LORE
Many other animal behaviors are erroneously used to forecast rain. So, don't bank on rain if:

- A pigeon washes.
- A sparrow chirps.
- A cat washes over its ears.
- A robin comes close to the house.
- A chicken rolls in the dust.

OAK BEFORE ASH, ONLY A SPLASH...

"Ash before oak, soak, soak, soak." The rhyme has long been used to predict the summer weather from the order in which these two trees come into leaf, but it is not a very reliable guide as the ash is almost always second of the two, whatever is to come.

Britain's Woodland Trust, using records dating back to the 18th century, endorses the dubious worth of this rhyme. Even though, unlike the oak, it bears its delicate sprays of tufted flowers before the leaves emerge, the ash is rarely in leaf before the oak. However British summers are growing hotter and drier, so it may be premature to write off the forecast altogether.

The English oak (*Quercus robur*) can live for well over 500 and reputedly as long as 1,000 years. Many oaks appear as landmarks on old maps, and long-felled trees, thought to be stopping points when the bounds of a parish were "beaten," live on in names such as Gospel Oak in North London.

The ash (*Fraxinus excelsior*), easy to recognize in winter from its black buds and silver-gray bark, is sometimes known as the Queen of the Forest and in Scandinavian mythology was called Yggdrasil, the tree of life.

While the strength of oak wood has long been prized for the weight-bearing timbers of houses and ships, ash combines both strength and elasticity, and is still the wood of choice for making crab and lobster pots. Ash is also prized as firewood, as it will burn when green, hence the saying: "Ash dry or ash green makes a fire fit for a queen."

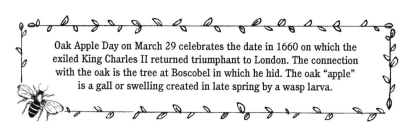

Oak Apple Day on March 29 celebrates the date in 1660 on which the exiled King Charles II returned triumphant to London. The connection with the oak is the tree at Boscobel in which he hid. The oak "apple" is a gall or swelling created in late spring by a wasp larva.

RAIN BEFORE SEVEN, FINE BY ELEVEN

An old English saying, and a good forecast of the weather in many other temperate locations, as long as you are liberal enough to take "seven" and "eleven" to mean early and late morning. It is certainly more reliable than its counterpart "fine before seven, rain by eleven."

This saying works because the weather that accompanies a depression is unlikely to last more than four to eight hours, and rainfall that begins the previous evening is likely to peter out before noon the next day. A depression or low pressure area is formed when masses of cold and warm air meet and the warm air rises over the cold. As a result, clouds develop and rain falls. If the pressure falls even more it becomes windy as air is sucked in because, as in the school rhyme: "winds always blow from high to low [pressure]."

On average a raindrop measures $\frac{1}{12}$ inch (2 mm) across.

Raindrops, technically "precipitation that reaches the ground in liquid form," result from the collision of droplets inside a turbulent cloud, making them large enough to fall to the ground. Alternatively, when supercooled water droplets and ice crystals exist together in a cloud, water droplets move towards and enlarge the ice crystals until they are large enough to fall. Whether they reach the ground as rain, sleet or snow depends on the air temperature.

According to a rhyme said to be by the 19th-century judge Baron Charles Bowen:

The rain it raineth every day
Upon the Just and Unjust fella,
But more upon the Just because
The unjust stole the Just's umbrella

AS THE DAYS LENGTHEN THE COLD STRENGTHENS

••

The conclusion is correct because, in northern latitudes, the sea continues to cool down after the winter solstice on December 21 and this has an effect on the weather. However the lowest temperatures do not necessarily occur on January 14, the date midway between the end of autumn and the beginning of spring.

Because the sea cools (and heats up) more slowly than the land, the weather generally continues to get colder right through January and February. This means that when cold air blows from the north – especially when high pressure systems bring Arctic winds south – there is nothing to temper its effects. Occasionally, however, "old wives' summers" – periods of unseasonably warm weather – occur in December and January. December 2015 was so warm in Britain that daffodils were in bloom before Christmas, while in the USA hundreds of weather records were broken in the 48 most southerly states. There can be little doubt that climate change is playing a significant part in these effects.

It is said that a January spring "isn't worth a pin" – in other words, it won't last and, even worse, can be bad for the crops, which overgrow or become "winter proud." It may also predict wet weather to come, as in the saying "January spring, February wring."

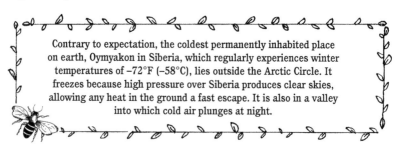

Contrary to expectation, the coldest permanently inhabited place on earth, Oymyakon in Siberia, which regularly experiences winter temperatures of −72°F (−58°C), lies outside the Arctic Circle. It freezes because high pressure over Siberia produces clear skies, allowing any heat in the ground a fast escape. It is also in a valley into which cold air plunges at night.

RED SKY AT NIGHT, SHEPHERD'S DELIGHT...

"Red sky in the morning, shepherd's (or sailor's) warning." Wherever the weather comes predominantly from the west, the first part of this saying is one of the most reliable weather forecasts, as long as you distinguish a benign red sky from a livid, angry one.

Colors in the sky arise from the dust and moisture in the atmosphere, which split and scatter the sun's light. At the beginning and end of the day, when sunlight travels farthest, the "long" red, orange and yellow rays of the spectrum are scattered least, and are therefore most visible. If, as the sun sets, the sky glows rosy pink, this signals dry air in the west, from where the next day's weather will arrive. Moisture in the atmosphere makes the light disperse differently, creating the vivid yellow or reddish-orange clouds that predict rain.

In the morning, a yellow sky also forecasts rain. If it is a livid red, then the chance of rain depends on the type of clouds and their extent. As the 19th-century forecaster CL Prince observed: "If at sunrise small reddish-looking clouds are seen low on the horizon, it must not always be considered to indicate rain... It has frequently been observed that if [the clouds] extend ten degrees, rain will follow before two or three p.m.; but if still higher and nearer the zenith [the point directly above an observer], rain will fall within three hours."

OTHER GOOD EARLY MORNING PREDICTIONS
For a rain-free day: Clouds driven away by the sunrise, gray sky to the east or a sea that is darker than the sky.
For rain to come: Dark clouds to the west, too bright a sky or a red sky, with the sun rising over a bank of cloud (a high dawn).

NEVER SMILE AT A CROCODILE

And don't get near one either – they can be deadly. Camouflaged to look like floating logs, with only their eyes and nostrils visible above the surface of the water, crocs lurk in the shallows waiting to sense the smells and vibrations of nearby prey.

The song in which this phrase was coined was written in 1952 by Jack Lawrence and Frank Churchill for the Walt Disney movie version of *Peter Pan*, which was released the following year. In the story, the crocodile – which ticks because it had swallowed a clock – terrorizes the villainous Captain Hook. The first verse goes:

Never smile at a crocodile
No you can't get friendly with a crocodile,
Don't be taken in by his welcome grin,
He's imagining how well you'll fit within his skin.

A crocodile strikes with sudden, awesome power, instinctively shaking its prey from side to side. Experts say that playing dead, which can prompt the animal to leave its victim under rocks or logs to eat later, provides a slim likelihood of surviving an attack. Poking the creature in the eye or pulling its tail are other last resorts.

In a real life horror story from 2011, Australian cruise ship hostess Tara Hawkes was attacked by a crocodile that lunged into her leg and began to pull her under the surface of the water in Dugong Bay. She was saved only

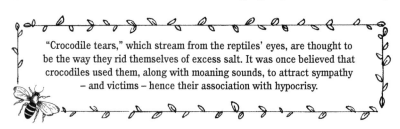

"Crocodile tears," which stream from the reptiles' eyes, are thought to be the way they rid themselves of excess salt. It was once believed that crocodiles used them, along with moaning sounds, to attract sympathy – and victims – hence their association with hypocrisy.

after her companion Al Sartori dived in and heroically jabbed his thumbs into the attacker's eyes, making the crocodile relax its grip.

To tell crocodiles and alligators apart, look at the teeth: in a crocodile at least one tooth is visible at the side of the head when the mouth is shut. Crocodiles – unlike alligators, which apart from the rare Chinese alligator live only in North and South America – inhabit tropical regions throughout the world.

DON'T EAT WILD BLACKBERRIES AFTER MICHAELMAS

Because, according to legend, on Michaelmas night, September 29, the feast of St. Michael the Archangel, the Devil spits or urinates on them. Certainly blackberries begin to lose their flavor at this time, when they are also likely to get damp and moldy or be affected by early frosts.

Seeds discovered by archaeologists in the stomachs of Neolithic human remains prove that Britons have been enjoying the juicy purple fruits of the blackberry (*Rubus fruticosus*) for over 4,000 years. And since medieval times blackberry leaves, infused in boiling water and with honey added, have been valued for treating inflammation of the mouth, and to soothe both digestive ills and the excruciating pain of gout.

Old recipes for blackberries include blackberry crowdie, made with oats, cream and rum, and bramble jelly. Paired with apples, they are the perfect ingredient for an autumn pie or crumble.

Known as "lawyers" because their thorny, arching stems are difficult to escape from once they entrap you, brambles were also commonly planted around graves, for the practical reason of deterring sheep and weeds; also to keep the dead in their place and the Devil out.

ON MAGPIES: ONE FOR SORROW, TWO FOR MIRTH

The magpie, with its striking black and white plumage and long tail, has long been a bird of ill omen. Its coloring is said by many to have come from its refusal to take on full black mourning after Christ's crucifixion.

According to long-held superstition, whether ill luck – or some other life-changing event – will befall you depends on how many magpies you see together. A more upbeat version begins:

One for sorrow, two for joy,
Three for a girl and four for a boy.

Or alternatively (though there are several more versions):

Three for a wedding, four for death,
Five for silver, six for gold,
Seven for a secret, not to be told,
Eight for heaven, nine for [Hell],
And ten for the D…l's own sell.

There are many traditional ways of dispelling the ill luck of seeing a single magpie. You should, some believe, bow and say aloud, "Good morning to you Mr. Magpie, Sir," or, "Good magpie, magpie, chatter and flee, turn up thy tail and good luck fall me." Others make great ceremony of removing their hats when a single magpie crosses their path; yet others will spit or make the sign of the cross on the ground.

Magpies will peck at windows, thinking that their own reflections are rival birds.

The magpie (*Pica pica*) is a close relative of the crow and except for Iceland breeds all over Europe. It is increasingly common near human habitations where it supplements its

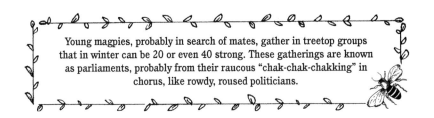

Young magpies, probably in search of mates, gather in treetop groups that in winter can be 20 or even 40 strong. These gatherings are known as parliaments, probably from their raucous "chak-chak-chakking" in chorus, like rowdy, roused politicians.

insect and grain diet with food scraps. The magpie's reputation for stealing is immortalized in Rossini's opera *La Gazza Ladra* (*The Thieving Magpie*) of 1817 in which a maid-servant is condemned to death for the bird's crime.

A CUCKOO IN SEPTEMBER, NO ONE EVER CAN REMEMBER

A tribute to the migratory habits of the cuckoo, although in some country districts people once believed that in the autumn cuckoos changed themselves into hawks in order to survive the winter at home in Britain.

This saying is the last line of a rhyme with several versions, one of which is:

Cuckoo, cuckoo, pray what do you do?
In April [Ap-er-il] I open my bill
In May I sing both night and noon
In June I change my tune
In July away I fly
In August away I must...

As the rhyme rightly relates, the call of the cuckoo (*Cuculus canorus*) is most persistent in early summer, then it changes subtly to a "cuk-cuck-oo"

195

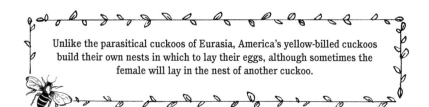

Unlike the parasitical cuckoos of Eurasia, America's yellow-billed cuckoos build their own nests in which to lay their eggs, although sometimes the female will lay in the nest of another cuckoo.

later in the season. The cuckoo is renowned as a brood parasite, laying its huge eggs in the nest of small birds, including meadow pipits and hedge sparrows. The eggs hatch into large young, which evict the rest of the clutch. Their massive gapes are irresistible to the rearing instincts of the foster parents, which spend from 17 to 21 exhausting days bringing food before the fledgling cuckoo flees the nest.

CUCKOO LORE
Like magpies, cuckoos are the objects of many superstitions:

- ☞ The number of consecutive calls you hear is the number of years until you marry.
- ☞ If you hear a cuckoo before the swallows have arrived, sorrow lies ahead for you.
- ☞ When you hear the first cuckoo, look under your shoe. You will find a hair the same color as that of your spouse-to-be.
- ☞ Whatever you are doing when you hear the first cuckoo you will continue to do all year.
- ☞ If you have money in your pocket when you hear the first cuckoo then you will have wealth all year.
- ☞ The luckiest time to hear a first cuckoo is on Easter morning.

HORSES SLEEP STANDING UP

They do – although they sleep lying down as well. This ability to stand and "power nap" allows horses to get the rest they need and to make a quick escape from predators if necessary.

Horses are able to doze standing up because they possess a stay apparatus, a system of ligaments and tendons that hold the creatures in a standing position while their muscles relax. They will spend 4–15 hours a day in "standing rest," while taking short naps totaling about two hours.

Like humans, horses experience sleep of different kinds. Their standing or slow wave sleep (named from brainwave frequency) is a shallow sleep. Only when they lie down can horses experience rapid eye movement (REM) sleep – the equivalent of our dreaming sleep. A horse needs comparatively little of this type of sleep, probably an hour or two a week, but without it is likely to become ill-tempered or neurotic.

The partnership between horse and humans goes back more than 6,000 years to the steppes where horses were kept for food and, before the invention of the wheel, became our first mode of transport.

Studies of horses show that they have more REM sleep when they live in groups, because one horse will stand sentinel while others relax in safety. Even in a comfortable stable a horse may feel isolated, confined – and wakeful – especially if it fears becoming "cast:" trapped against a wall with insufficient room to get to its feet if danger threatens.

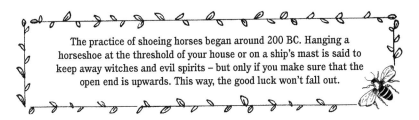

The practice of shoeing horses began around 200 BC. Hanging a horseshoe at the threshold of your house or on a ship's mast is said to keep away witches and evil spirits – but only if you make sure that the open end is upwards. This way, the good luck won't fall out.

WHEN ROOKS BUILD LOW, IT'S A SIGN OF A WET SUMMER TO COME

Rooks are sociable birds that nest in rookeries, which at their largest consist of several thousand pairs. But rooks' flight patterns are usually better weather forecasters than their building habits.

Because rooks return to the same place year after year, and because rookeries consist of many renovated old nests as well as some new ones, it is virtually impossible to link nest height with the coming weather. More significant to rook well-being is the rookery's strict pecking order, with the oldest male bird at the centre, sheltered from the wind.

In the autumn, a male rook finds a nesting spot and sings to his partner, brings her food, then bows and calls to her before they begin together to make or renovate an untidy nest. Females will fight fiercely over building materials, fending off thieves. Sentries posted at the edge of the colony or parliament while chicks are being fed will warn when danger threatens.

Country people believe it is lucky to have a rookery near their house. If rooks suddenly leave, this is a sign that a death has occurred.

When rooks "tumble" through the air, it is said that rain is on the way, while rooks that twist and turn after leaving the nest are believed to forecast storms. Weather observers give these forecasts a reliability rating of 70 percent. A very noisy rookery is also said to presage unsettled weather.

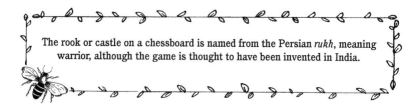

The rook or castle on a chessboard is named from the Persian *rukh*, meaning warrior, although the game is thought to have been invented in India.

THE DEEPER THE CLOUD, THE HARDER IT SHOWERS

This good forecast is based on the reliable association between heavy rainfall and the appearance of towering cumulonimbus clouds in the sky. When the sun emerges between the clouds and the showers a rainbow may arch across the sky.

Cumulus clouds are heaped, but cumulonimbus are towering, mountainous ones, named from the Latin *nimbus*, meaning rain. The base is usually dark and the top is either wispy and fibrous, where water is freezing into ice crystals, or flattened into an anvil shape. From clouds like this, heavy "hard" showers may easily develop into full-scale thunderstorms.

Cumulonimbus clouds develop only when the air is deeply unstable and mostly in summer when upward air currents are strongest. They form quickly and are usually short-lived. Once they have dropped their payload of rain – or hail or snow – they may quickly peter out.

Tornado alert: if pendulous breast-like blobs of cloud hang from the underside of the anvil (described as cumulonimbus with mammatus) a severe thunderstorm is imminent, and possibly even a tornado.

A cumulonimbus cloud with an anvil top is known as a cumulonimbus incus. The largest of these, which are especially common in the tropics, can reach 6 miles (10 km) in height – higher than Mount Everest. Ahead of a very severe storm you may see the top of the anvil bulge. This is caused by an updraft of air carrying a parcel of cloud into the stratosphere.

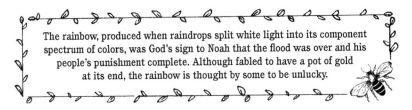

The rainbow, produced when raindrops split white light into its component spectrum of colors, was God's sign to Noah that the flood was over and his people's punishment complete. Although fabled to have a pot of gold at its end, the rainbow is thought by some to be unlucky.

NEVER KILL A RAVEN

Especially if it lives at the Tower of London, where ravens are protected by royal decree. Traditionally ravens are afforded respect, for as well as being birds of wit and wisdom their voices are deemed to be deathly omens.

In London ravens have guarded the Tower for centuries. In response to complaints by the Astronomer Royal, John Flamsteed (1646–1719), that the birds' activities were marring his observations, Charles II ordered their destruction. But to fulfil the prophecy that the absence of ravens would mean the fall of the monarchy, six were saved. Today, as insurance against accident and illness, seven or eight birds are kept.

LEGENDARY RAVENS
Many legends surround the omnivorous raven (*Corvus corax*), the world's largest all-black songbird:

☞ In the Bible, ravens brought food to the wilderness for the prophet Elijah.
☞ The fluttering of ravens is said to have warned the Roman orator Cicero of his impending death.
☞ According to the legends of the Pacific Northwest, the raven was the creator of the world and bringer of daylight.
☞ In Swedish legend, ravens are the ghosts of murdered men.
☞ When the raven croaks, beware; for when it says "corpse, corpse" people will sicken and die.
☞ Ravens can smell death and are associated in history with places of execution where, after observing the proceedings, they would peck at discarded bodies.

Ravens mate for life and have been known to live for over 40 years. They are much bigger than crows and have fatter beaks. They are depicted in the prehistoric cave paintings at Lascaux in France. Grip, Barnaby's pet raven in Charles Dickens's novel *Barnaby Rudge*, perfectly expresses the birds' character and chattering voice when he says: "Halloa halloa halloa. What's the matter here! Keep up your spirits. Never say die! Bow wow wow. I'm a devil, I'm a devil."

ELEPHANTS NEVER FORGET

Close scientific studies of elephant herds prove this to be true. These remarkable creatures not only memorize information essential to their survival but also seem to mourn their dead.

In the elephant family herd, which can number up to 20 females and their young (both male and female), the memory of the senior female, the matriarch, is crucial. It is she who remembers the location of fruitful food sources and reliable waterholes, even those located beneath desiccated mud. She also knows where danger lies and all the females in the group will clearly remember the distinctive smells of hyenas, lions and other predators.

The result of elephants' powerful memories are "elephant roads," tracks that often penetrate dense forest and are used for generations. When a matriarch dies a mature female, often her oldest surviving daughter, takes over the leadership and she, too, will remember routes taken regularly since she was a calf.

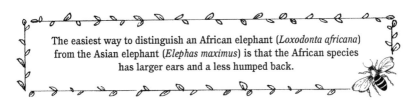

The easiest way to distinguish an African elephant (*Loxodonta africana*) from the Asian elephant (*Elephas maximus*) is that the African species has larger ears and a less humped back.

An elephant herd will often break into smaller groups, especially when food is scarce. On reuniting, the animals greet each other noisily, touching each other with their trunks. When an animal is ill the others in the herd cluster around, trumpeting their distress. If a mother elephant loses her calf she will stay with her dead infant, chasing off predators. And when they encounter the bones of a carcass, elephants will stop to touch them, as if in mourning, and even carry them off into the bushes.

ELEPHANT LANGUAGE
Rogue elephant – an aggressive individual living away from the herd.
Pink elephant – a hallucinatory animal seen only by the inebriated.
White elephant – an object of no use other than to give away.
Elephant and Castle – a part of London, but originally the name of a pub deriving from the ancient habit of placing a howdah or "castle" on the back of a war elephant.
Elephant's foot – an African relative of the yam with a root resembling an elephant's foot.

THE FOX MAY GROW GRAY, BUT NEVER GOOD

This saying epitomizes the cunning of the fox and its reputation as a wily hunter that does not change its ways, even with age. The creature features in folklore from around the world as a cunning trickster.

The face of the fox (*Vulpes vulpes*), with its pointed, slender nose – equipped with an acute sense of smell – sharp eyes and pricked ears, is the picture of cleverness. But its penchant for poultry, and its

According to folklore, a fox gets rid of fleas in its fur by taking a leaf in its mouth, then walking backwards into water until it is entirely submerged, making the fleas either move on to the leaf or be drowned.

instinct for killing more birds than it could ever eat, makes this wily animal the farmer's enemy. It is rumoured that a fox will carry off a goose from the farmyard with the head in its mouth and the body slung over its shoulder.

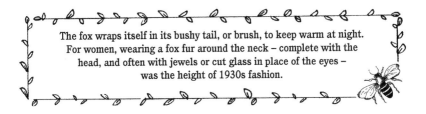

The fox wraps itself in its bushy tail, or brush, to keep warm at night. For women, wearing a fox fur around the neck – complete with the head, and often with jewels or cut glass in place of the eyes – was the height of 1930s fashion.

Although long and vigorously hunted as a pest and for sport, the fox continues to thrive in both country and town through its adaptability, opportunism and cunning. When chased by hounds, foxes will dive into one of many "earths," backtrack on their own trails, walk along the tops of fences and even run through flocks of sheep.

In towns, foxes thrive anywhere food is on tap from rubbish bags or dustbins (they push the lids off with their noses), and will make earths for breeding and raising cubs in secluded spots in parks and gardens – even under wooden decking where they may accumulate piles of wrapping from discarded fast food remains. If you catch an animal's eyes in your headlights and they shine white or blue then you've most probably encountered a fox.

In American folklore the trickster fox was popularized as Brer Fox in the *Uncle Remus* tales by Joel Chandler Harris (1848–1908). Based on both European and African-American traditions, he is outclassed in wit and wiliness by his companion Brer Rabbit.

A BUTTERFLY LIVES FOR JUST ONE DAY

An exaggerated claim: without becoming a meal for a bird or bat, and allowed to fulfil its natural span, the minimum lifetime of a butterfly is about a week. But some butterflies, especially those that hibernate or migrate, can live for a year or more.

For a butterfly, food is a major factor in determining lifespan. As a general rule (though not infallibly), butterflies that feed solely on nectar – a high sugar but short-lived energy source – live for only two to four weeks. Butterflies of this kind include the papilios, a large group to which the swallowtails belong. Longer-lived butterflies, such as the beautiful heliconid butterflies of Central and South America and the clearwings of Costa Rica, which can live for up to 13 months, feed on both nectar and pollen, a diet that provides more sustained energy.

While most die at the end of summer, some butterflies, including the richly colored peacocks (*Inachis io*) with distinctive "eyes" on their

In the mid 1960s, at the height of his prowess in the ring, the late boxer Muhammad Ali coined the catchphrase "Float like a butterfly, sting like a bee."

wings, hibernate over the winter months in sheds and outhouses. On mild winter days they may emerge briefly. If so they should be left alone and discouraged from flying out into the open – to their deaths.

Of all long-lived butterflies, most remarkable are the orange and black monarchs (*Danaus plexippus*) of the northern USA and southern Canada. Adults that emerge in spring have a lifespan of only a few weeks but those emerging later migrate by the million to California, Mexico and Florida. Here they cluster in huge groups on "butterfly trees" used year after year (and probably located by smell) by new generations of adults.

After early spring mating the males die and the females head north, then lay their eggs on milkweed (*Asclepias* spp) before they too die. The caterpillars – an unmistakable green with yellow and white stripes – feed day and night on the milkweed then, like all butterflies, change into chrysalises from which newly metamorphosed adults emerge.

WHEN THE SCARLET PIMPERNEL CLOSES IT'S GOING TO RAIN

Not for nothing is this small, bright red flower known as the poor man's weatherglass, change-of-the-weather, shepherd's sundial and weather flower. It will invariably close its petals if the sky becomes overcast ahead of rain.

The scarlet pimpernel (*Anagallis arvensis*), a common weed of gardens, waste ground and dunes, is not, however, an all-day forecaster. For whatever the weather it will have closed its petals by 2:00 p.m. and will keep them shut until 8:00 a.m. If the petals open fully in the morning a fine day can be expected. But the reverse is not true. When the flowers fail to open first thing it is likely to remain cloudy, but the chance of rainfall is little better than about 15 percent.

Like the scarlet pimpernel, other flowers, including daisies (*Bellis* spp) and bindweeds (*Convolvulus* spp) close when the day is damp because the cells at the base of the petals detect and respond to increasing levels of moisture in the air. When they close towards the end of the day the petals are responding to lowering levels of sunlight.

The Scarlet Pimpernel (Sir Peter Blakeney), the elusive fictional character, created by Baroness Orczy (1865–1947), was named from his use of the little red flower as his emblem.

The 18th-century Swedish botanist Carolus Linneaus, known as the father of taxonomy, devised a famous floral timepiece, "a clock by which one could tell the time, even in cloudy weather, as accurately as by a watch," based on the specific times at which some flowers open and close each day. As he observed, "The Crepis [hawksbeard] began to open its flowers at 6:00 a.m., and they were fully open by 6:30. The Leontodon [hawkbit] opened all its flowers between 6:00 and 7:00 a.m...." The scarlet pimpernel occupied the eight o'clock position.

A SWARM OF BEES IN MAY IS WORTH A LOAD OF HAY...

"A swarm of bees in June is worth a silver spoon. A swarm of bees in July is not worth a fly." Or in other words, by late summer the value of the swarm is minimal.

Honey bees (*Apis mellifera*) swarm to increase their numbers. In early summer the young queens are ready to fly from the hive, or from wild colonies established in old buildings or hollow trees. At the same time the workers become restless: they gather at the hive entrance, then go back in again to raid the honey cells for food.

When a new queen emerges, about half the workers first cluster,

BEE MYTHS
No doubt because of their value, bees feature in
many other superstitions:

✍ If you dream of bees, you have unknown enemies trying to do
you some mischief.
✍ If a swarm settles on the roof of a house or the dead branch of
a tree, it is a sign of death.
✍ It is also a sign of death if a swarm comes down the chimney.
✍ Do not drive a bee out of the house: you will drive out good luck.
✍ To keep your bees, and to stop them stinging, inform the bees
of a forthcoming wedding – and leave them a piece of cake.
✍ When someone dies, tell the bees and put the hive into
mourning with black ribbons; otherwise they too will die and
will no longer bring you good luck.

then swarm, around her as she flies off. If the queen has already been
impregnated by a drone the swarm will seek a new home. If not, she may
return to the hive she has just left, in which case any remaining unfertilized
queens will be killed by the worker bees.

During the summer a colony of honey bees consists of about 50,000
workers (sterile females) a few hundred drones (males) and one queen. The
workers make the honey, which sustains them and which they feed to the
queen and the drones over the winter. Of the 440 pounds (200 kg) or more
of honey that a colony may produce, only about a third is used by the bees
themselves. And the better use the swarm makes of the profusion of early
summer flowers, the more honey they make.

A SWAN CAN BREAK YOUR ARM WITH A WING BEAT

This is usually untrue, although a wounded American swan once broke a hunter's arm and an angry swan can inflict a nasty bruise. In Britain all swans on the River Thames belong, by law, to the Queen, or to one of two London livery companies.

The amazing transformation of the dowdy brown cygnet into a handsome adult in Hans Christian Andersen's 19th-century fairy tale The Ugly Duckling *is believed to be autobiographical in its inspiration.*

Like all other birds, the swan has hollow bones that help to make it light enough to fly. This means that if it attacks something as solid as a human arm, the bird bones are the more likely to break. But attack it will, for swans are highly territorial and defend their nests, eggs and chicks (cygnets), using bony projections on their extended wings as weapons. Mute swans certainly kill both other swans and Canada geese, probably by drowning them.

Britain's most common swan, and its only permanent resident, is the mute swan (*Cygnus olor*), which in fact makes a whole variety of hissing, snorting, snoring and strangled trumpeting sounds. The American swan (*C. americanus*), a close relative of the Bewick (*C. colombianus bewickii*), which visits Britain in winter and is named for the famous bird illustrator Thomas Bewick (1753–1828), migrates south from the Arctic tundra as far

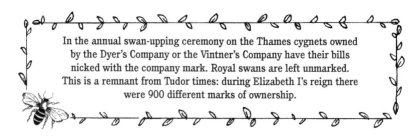

In the annual swan-upping ceremony on the Thames cygnets owned by the Dyer's Company or the Vintner's Company have their bills nicked with the company mark. Royal swans are left unmarked. This is a remnant from Tudor times: during Elizabeth I's reign there were 900 different marks of ownership.

as Chesapeake Bay. Its feathers have long been prized for warm bonnets. The black swan (*C. atratus*), native to Australia and introduced into New Zealand, is a gregarious bird living in flocks of up to 50,000.

The world's oldest swannery is at Abbotsbury in Dorset, where birds are tended by a swanherd. The post goes back to the Middle Ages, when swans were kept for food and regularly served as a delicacy at banquets.

IVY CAN PULL A HOUSE DOWN

Maybe not literally, but it can do serious damage if it penetrates cracks or crevices in weakened bricks or the mortar between them. Nor will it often kill a tree, although it may weaken one by depriving it of water and nutrients.

The ivy (*Hedera helix*) clings to its support, whether living or not, with "bearded" stems. The beards are in fact overground or aerial roots, which the plant uses to suck up additional moisture and dissolved minerals. Ivy can be so vigorous that it can grow to the height of a three-storey house or a mature tree, producing its own trunks up to a foot (30 cm) across.

According to legend ivy will prevent drunkenness, a belief that derives from the fact that it can easily smother a grapevine.

As ivy matures the leaves change in shape from triangular to diamond-shaped. It produces its pale green flowers late in the year and even on a sunny winter day you can see it buzzing with hungry insects relishing the energy-packed pollen. Beekeepers have long appreciated the value of ivy in topping up insects' winter supplies of both nectar and pollen.

ALL ABOUT IVY
Ivy has long country associations with health, love and luck:

☞ Ivy leaves will charm away warts and verrucas.
☞ Give ivy to a ewe after birthing to restore her appetite.
☞ Gather ivy and give it to cattle before noon on Christmas Day
   and the Devil will stay away for a year.
☞ Place an ivy wreath on a grave on All Saints' Day
   (November 1) to keep a soul safe.
☞ If a girl tucks an ivy leaf down her bosom the next man who
   speaks to her will be her own true love.
☞ To cure children of whooping cough, feed them from a bowl
   made of ivy wood.

THE LOUDER THE FROG, THE MORE THE RAIN

Frogs definitely perk up and "sing" more forcefully when the air is damp, whether or not rain is on the way. It is the males that have the loud voices – they employ them in the mating season to attract a female partner.

It is a truth of amphibian life that a moist skin is essential for activity, which is why frogs prefer being in damp places when they are on land. The frog's croak, used to attract a fertile female, reaches a loud boom in the bullfrog (*Rana catesbeina*), whose voice is amplified by large resonating sacs at the side of its throat. By contrast, the common frog (*R. temporaria*), widespread in Europe, has a deep, rasping croak. The females reply with softer chirrups and grunts.

Frogs are good for the garden: as well as insects they consume large quantities of slugs and snails (shells included) as well as insects of all kinds. Flying insects are caught on the sticky tip of the long tongue, which is attached at the front of the mouth and quickly thrust out towards passing prey.

The edible European frog most favored by French gastronomes is *R. esculenta*. According to the renowned French chef Auguste Escoffier (1846–1935) they are best poached in white wine, then steeped in a fish sauce with paprika and finally set into champagne jelly "to counterfeit the effect of water." Preceding this last stage, Escoffier recommended arranging sprigs of chervil and tarragon between the legs to resemble grass.

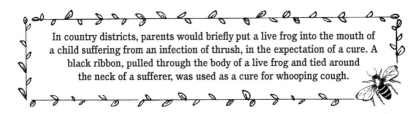

In country districts, parents would briefly put a live frog into the mouth of a child suffering from an infection of thrush, in the expectation of a cure. A black ribbon, pulled through the body of a live frog and tied around the neck of a sufferer, was used as a cure for whooping cough.

THE EARLY BIRD CATCHES THE WORM

An exhortation against lying abed and the folly of missed opportunities – and also a sound observation of both bird and worm behavior, despite the fact that in winter earthworms burrow too far down in the soil for even the most persistent birds to reach.

With endless energy earthworms till the soil, bringing subsoil to the surface from a depth of about 12–18 inches (30–40 cm) below ground, but sometimes from as much as 8 feet (2.4 m), grinding lumps of soil and ejecting them from their guts, and pulling leaves and

Birds sing at dawn to attract a mate but remain invisible to predators. Early singing also allows maximum time for feeding later in the day.

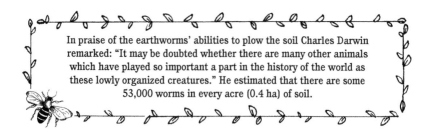

In praise of the earthworms' abilities to plow the soil Charles Darwin remarked: "It may be doubted whether there are many other animals which have played so important a part in the history of the world as these lowly organized creatures." He estimated that there are some 53,000 worms in every acre (0.4 ha) of soil.

other organic matter from the surface. Because earthworms are nocturnal, the early bird may catch them before they retire below ground at dawn.

When resting, worms lie vertically, head uppermost, below the surface of the ground. When they emerge from their burrows to feed their presence is detected by birds with keen eyesight. The blackbird (usually first to break into song in a city dawn chorus) will tilt its head to detect worms, which it pulls out unceremoniously with its strong, sharp beak. Its behavior is perfected to look for worms, not hear them – it tilts simply because its eyes are on the sides of its head. Thrushes and robins also enjoy worms, but no birds consume as many as nocturnal mammals – moles, hedgehogs and foxes.

The vigilant bird will also be on the alert after a rain shower, which brings earthworms to the surface. While dry leaves get stuck in the worms' burrows wet ones don't, so when the creatures sense rain they come to the surface for easy-to-use material. The moist air also means that they are able to move around on the surface without dehydrating.

CATS ALWAYS FALL ON THEIR FEET

Remarkably, they do. Using a combination of instinctive reactions and rapid movements they can right themselves in seconds, adding to their remarkable abilities to survive danger.

It is a fact of life that cats – and other animals too – need to be the right way up to function properly and, if placed on their backs, will struggle to

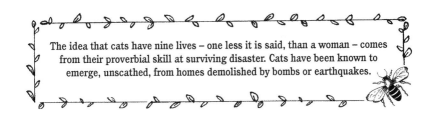

The idea that cats have nine lives – one less it is said, than a woman – comes from their proverbial skill at surviving disaster. Cats have been known to emerge, unscathed, from homes demolished by bombs or earthquakes.

re-orientate themselves. The marvel of the cat is that it rights itself with such speed and agility. Essential to the righting movements are the animal's well-developed senses of vision and balance, the latter controlled via the fluid in the labyrinth of the inner ear, which by its continuous movement informs the creature of its positioning instant by instant.

Slow-motion filming confirms that a falling cat performs a set sequence of movements. First the body is bent from the "waist" at an angle of 90°, with the front limbs kept close to the head and the hind legs splayed out from the trunk. Next the front part of the body is rotated through 180°, bringing the forelimbs vertical to the ground. Finally the back part of the body is rotated and the cat is the right way up with legs extended ready for a perfect landing.

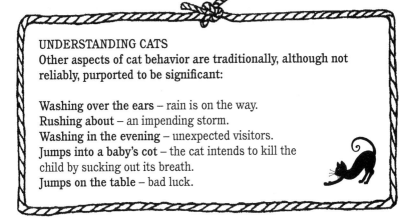

UNDERSTANDING CATS
Other aspects of cat behavior are traditionally, although not reliably, purported to be significant:

Washing over the ears – rain is on the way.
Rushing about – an impending storm.
Washing in the evening – unexpected visitors.
Jumps into a baby's cot – the cat intends to kill the child by sucking out its breath.
Jumps on the table – bad luck.

MOTHS COME OUT ONLY AT NIGHT

Most moths are indeed nocturnal – but by no means all. Luckily for the enthusiast many day-flying moths are superbly colored, their bright hues often advertising to birds the fact that they are poisonous.

Of all the world's day-flying moths one of the most spectacular is the humming-bird hawk moth (*Macroglossum stellatarum*). The moth, common in eastern Asia and across southern Europe, reaches southern Britain in large numbers in warm summers. Just like its avian namesake it hovers over flowers, sipping nectar from blooms such as phloxes and verbenas with its long proboscis and darting from one flower to the next. If your hearing is acute enough you may also be able to detect the high-pitched noise of its wing beats.

The caterpillars of the Isabella tiger moth (Pyrrharctia isabella) *are called woolly bears because they are small, dark and covered in bristles.*

Night-flying moths are mostly drab in color and though inconspicuous (many look very like leaves) can often be seen on vegetation during daylight hours. They use their powerful sense of smell to locate nectar. Unlike butterflies, which usually hold their wings together at 90° to their bodies, most moths lay their wings out flat when at rest. Look, too, for the typical feathery moth antennae, which contrast with butterflies' knob-tipped antennae.

The day-flying five-spot burnet moth (*Zygaena trifolii*), whose gray wings are splashed with scarlet, is a species that birds learn to avoid. The moths' bodies contain cyanide, which is formed from food by the caterpillars and transmitted to the adult during metamorphosis.

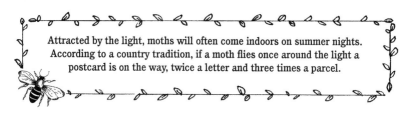

Attracted by the light, moths will often come indoors on summer nights. According to a country tradition, if a moth flies once around the light a postcard is on the way, twice a letter and three times a parcel.

DEW BEFORE MIDNIGHT, TOMORROW WILL BE BRIGHT

This saying is reliable because dew tends to form when the air is moist but skies are clear. According to the ancient Greeks dewdrops were the tears of Eos, the goddess of dawn.

The formation of dew depends, critically, on the temperatures of both the air and the ground, and the amount of moisture in the air. Also crucial is the dew point, the temperature at which the air, when cooled, will just become saturated with water vapor. So if on an early autumn evening the dew point is, say, 46°F (8°C), and the ground is still a warm 54°F (12°C), no dew will form. But once the ground temperature drops to 45°F (7°C), the water in the air will begin to condense, forming dewdrops.

Many dogs have rudimentary inner toes, known as dew claws, which need to be trimmed. The Saint Bernard has two sets of dew claws on the hind feet.

Artificial clay-lined "dew ponds," designed to collect water for grazing animals, were first dug in prehistoric times and later by gangs of laborers. They always contain some water, but in fact are largely filled by rain. Some water condenses into them from mist or fog, however, and their contents are added to by dew that runs off marginal plants.

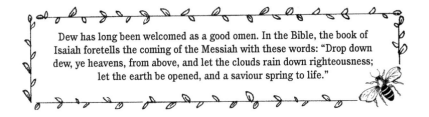

Dew has long been welcomed as a good omen. In the Bible, the book of Isaiah foretells the coming of the Messiah with these words: "Drop down dew, ye heavens, from above, and let the clouds rain down righteousness; let the earth be opened, and a saviour spring to life."

INDEX

THE AUTHOR

Ruth Binney has been collecting sayings and old wives' tales, and studying nature and the countryside, for over 50 years. She holds a degree in Natural Sciences from Cambridge University and has been involved in countless publications during her career as an editor. She is the author of many successful natural history and nostalgia titles, including the *Wise Words and Country Ways* and *Amazing and Extraordinary Facts* books, and *Plant Lore and Legend* (2016). She lives in Dorchester, England. **www.ruthbinney.com**